POCKET YOUR

ASSERTING
YOURSELF

Also available in this series

Coping with stress
Controlling your weight
Beating depression

POCKET YOUR PROBLEMS

ASSERTING YOURSELF

Dr Marsha Linehan and Dr Kelly Egan

Illustrated by Mel Calman

Introduced by
Virginia Ironside of Woman magazine

CENTURY PUBLISHING
LONDON

This book was devised and produced
by Multimedia Publications (UK) Ltd

Editors *Anne Cope and Christopher Fagg*
Design *Mike Spike*
Index *Anne Hardy*

First published in Great Britain in 1983
by Century Publishing Co. Ltd,
76 Old Compton Street, London W1V 5PA

ISBN 0 7126 0084 1 (paperback)
0 7126 0207 0 (cased)

Printed in Great Britain by
The Anchor Press Ltd, Tiptree, Essex

Contents

Introduction

As we grow older we quite naturally accumulate a fund of social knowledge. I am not talking about etiquette or savoir faire, but about knowing intuitively which social manoeuvres work and make us feel good. We learn that profuse apologies or excuses leave a sour taste; that we can tell people too much about ourselves at a first meeting; that saying No does not damage a relationship provided we say it promptly and without rancour. But it takes a lot of social encounters, and usually a lot of mistakes, to acquire such knowledge.

That is why a book like this is so useful. The authors, who have many years of social research and counselling between them, give innumerable short-cuts to social success. Here are lots of examples, confirmed by some intriguing pieces of research, of techniques and attitudes that are effective, whether one defines effectiveness as getting the things you want, making the relationships you want, or simply keeping your self-respect.

A large proportion of the letters in my postbag come from people who are too shy to stand up for themselves, too nervous to make conversation at parties, too fearful of rejection to ask for dates . . . They see their inability to cope as a moral failure, as a sign that they are, in some fundamental way, unlikeable and stupid. But shyness is only a *social* failure. A shy person is not a failure as a person. Would it be reasonable to regard yourself as an all-round failure if you failed your driving test? Of course it wouldn't.

As behaviourists Drs Linehan and Egan believe that most social difficulties are due to a lack or misuse of social skills. Like other skills, social skills are learned. By the same token inappropriate social skills can be unlearned. All social encounters can be teased apart and analysed, and there are usually good reasons why a particular encounter is unsuccessful. The first step is to analyse why. Having done that one can start to improve things. This usually involves gradual relearning, either informally or formally with professional help. And the beauty of learning social skills is that they are so soon rewarded—with smiles, laughs, respect, friendship.

Like everything else we learn—cooking, driving, playing the piano—practice is essential. No one is born a 'natural' cook. I'd hate to be driven by a 'natural' driver who had never had a lesson!

I particularly admire the authors' candour when they admit that there are social situations in which, no matter how good one's skills, the cards are dealt all wrong. Indeed, a large part of social competence lies in being able to choose and influence situations so that they work to your advantage. Again, that sort of judgement demands a clear analysis. The authors end with sound advice about seeking professional help. Do you know the difference between growth groups, social skills classes and therapy? The authors explain fully the strengths of all these options.

Of course, no one wants to conduct their social life by the book—'Ah! This is the situation described on page 18'. But if you know that social encounters have goals and rules—and that you can apply this knowledge if spontaneity goes wrong—you will, in the end, be able to perform all sorts of acts on your social trapeze.

Virginia Ironside

Authors' Preface

Until quite recently, mental health professionals worked within a rather negative model of human problems. People who approached them for help were usually thought to have something 'wrong' with them, and the therapist's role was to 'remove' this and make the person well again. This model is similar to that used by doctors in treating the sick: remove the disease and health will follow. One result of this way of thinking was that mental health workers had little connection with psychologists who studied 'normal' behaviour; a second was that they had very little knowledge of how to teach new behaviour; and a third, very important, result was that people seeking help for their problems were stigmatized by the idea that they had something 'wrong' with them (although it was never very clear what this something was). This meant that many people who sincerely wanted to change something about themselves hesitated to seek help.

Gradually, however, things are changing, and an 'educational' and 'skills' model of human problems is taking over from a 'disease' and 'treatment' model. This means that the therapist's job is seen more often now as the teaching of new skills, rather than the removal of not very well defined 'illnesses'. Several factors are responsible for this change. Firstly, it was becoming clear that the old model simply did not work—people often did not 'improve' when 'treatment' was applied. Secondly, academic and research psychologists became more interested in people's problems, particularly problems of social behaviour; this led to a closing of the gap between clinical and academic psychologists and to a vast amount of research on a subject previously thought to be outside the realm of academic psychologists. This research has shown very clearly that the principles which underlie 'normal' behaviour also apply to 'abnormal' behaviour. It has also become clear that the two types of behaviour are not as separate as was once thought, but that they merge imperceptibly into one another. There is thus no question of calling some people 'normal' and others 'abnormal'—all of us at times behave in ways which are inappropriate, unskilled, or strange.

These findings raised some exciting possibilities. If 'normal' behaviour is learned, then so is 'abnormal' behaviour. And, if behaviour is learned, then it can be 'unlearned' and more skilled, adaptive behaviour learned instead. There is now a great deal of evidence to support these ideas. Clinical psychologists, that is, psychologists who specialize in helping people to change their behaviour, have gradually found their research overlapping more and more with that of social psychologists, psychologists who are interested in how people interact with each other in social situations—it is in our social environment that most learning takes place. This 'marriage' is illustrated in much of the research we discuss in this book.

The idea that the task of a therapist is to teach new skills makes virtually all of us candidates for therapeutic intervention; there are very few people who would not benefit from some improvement in their social behaviour. But as it is neither feasible nor desirable for all of us to rush to therapists, psychologists have devised many techniques which people can put into practice by themselves in order to change their behaviour.

If it comes as a surprise to the reader to find that social behaviour is nowhere discussed in relation to personality, then this is perhaps the place to state our philosophical position. When psychologists talk about personality, what they are actually describing is a person's habitual behaviour: an 'extrovert' is someone who habitually goes out a lot and gets on well with a lot of people, whereas an 'introvert' habitually stays at home and dislikes noisy gatherings. But it cannot be said that either personality type *causes* these behaviours—personality is simply *inferred from* these behaviours. When so-called introverts receive therapy, they are almost always observed to become more extroverted, or rather their score on any one of a number of personality tests changes, because their behaviour has changed. Increasingly, social psychologists are recognizing that environment is the crucial and controlling factor in behaviour; certain environments may of course lead to the formation of certain behaviour habits which it is convenient to label 'extrovert' or 'introvert', but these habits are not the result of an innate or fixed entity called personality. What we familiarly call personality is no more than a set of habits which change as our situation changes. It is also a matter of common observation that this repertoire of habits becomes less fluid as we get older, because our receptivity to new experiences, and the incentive and motivation to seek new experiences, decline with age . . . not as a matter of biological fact, but because we assume and indeed expect that this should be so. There is no reason why a person should not 'grow' and change constantly throughout his or her life; only expectations and assumptions, and sometimes ignorance, stand in the way of enriching change.

As clinical psychologists, we believe that change is possible both in an individual's behaviour and in the way that individual typically interprets and responds to situations. Even those situations in which you habitually respond with certain behaviours, thoughts and attitudes are subject to change through conscious effort. Frequently, when a person comes into therapy with one of us, that person is convinced that he or she has a certain kind of personality. 'That's just the way I am; I can't help it,' they might say. One of the first tasks of therapy for such individuals is to help them come to a belief in their own ability to make changes in themselves and in their lives. Just because things have been a certain way in the past does not mean that they will always be that way.

Problems of social skill present themselves in many guises, and this is perhaps one of the reasons why it has taken psychologists so long to realize their importance. These examples will give some idea of what we mean.

A woman complains that she is depressed in spite of being happily married and enjoying a good job. It may take a therapist a number of sessions to work out that this woman's problem is a lack of the assertive skills necessary to get her husband to help more around the home. Having no idea how to tackle this important problem without damaging her marriage, she has given up trying. What at first glance may seem inexplicable depression is really a problem of social skills and can only be solved by teaching them.

A young man, an only child, has never found it easy to make friends. He is very sensitive to criticism and has gradually come to believe that others are constantly looking at him and making fun of him. This may or may not be true, but since he never mixes, he is unlikely to find out. Gradually, the idea that people are watching him and talking about him becomes stronger and, by the time he comes to the attention of the mental health professional, his 'paranoia' may be so marked that it obscures the basic social problem.

An overweight woman says that she desperately wants to lose weight so that she will be able to go out with men more often and be comfortable in social situations. Close questioning and observations of her daily activities and eating patterns reveals that, although she is quite active and sticks to low-calorie diets, she still does not lose very much weight. Whenever she goes back to eating a normal amount of food, she quickly regains her weight. After several sessions, it is determined that she falls into that group of fat people whose bodies tenaciously defend a body set weight much higher than people in our society find attractive in women. Because she has always, incorrectly, thought that her fat was due to her lack of willpower, or a secret unconscious desire to be fat, she has avoided being around attractive men. And even when she is around them, she dresses and acts as if she is unattractive and undesirable. Rather than express herself openly and freely, she retreats into the background or hides her interest in other people.

These everyday but complicated examples should not be taken to imply that everyone who is depressed or overweight is deficient in social skills. Nor do they imply that all social problems masquerade in this way. Often, we know only too well when our social behaviour is the problem. Unfortunately, and for reasons we will discuss in later chapters, it can be very difficult to work out exactly what the problem *is*. Or, we may blame other people for being hostile or unco-operative without realizing that our own behaviour has something to do with it. As a result, problems of social skills are often formulated in very unhelpful ways. The dictum 'I feel bored' may be an accurate statement of one's feelings, but it does nothing to help solve the problem of boredom. Often, it is this inability to pinpoint what is causing the problem that leads people to seek professional help, rather than the seriousness of the problem as such.

What do people with 'social' problems—and in one situation or another this is all of us—usually complain of? The most common general complaint is some variant of 'I don't like meeting people' or 'I don't make friends easily' or 'People don't seem to take to me'. Expressed like this, it is little wonder that no solution presents itself! Broken down more specifically, the complaint may become 'I don't know what to say when I meet people for the first time' or 'I've no small talk' or 'Men (or women) never ask me out twice/accept a second invitation'. Other common statements which imply that the speaker has some problem of social skills would be:

My children never obey me.
I find people very pushy.
My wife/husband and I are always quarrelling.
I wish my partner was a more considerate lover.
Why can't people tell when I mean 'No'?

No one listens to me.
I'm bored.
People never laugh at my jokes.
I can't seem to get really close to anyone.

Many of these statements, of course, might imply some problem in the situation: the person who never gets a laugh may be surrounded by extremely serious people; the warring couple may be better off apart. We hope, at least, that when you have read this book, you will be able to tell the difference!

Marsha Linehan and Kelly Egan

1

There's no getting away from people

Wishing to be friends is quick work, but friendship is a slow-ripening fruit.

ARISTOTLE (384–322 BC)

Some individuals seem to be more successful in dealing with people than others. They can influence people when necessary, but they are also well liked and have close, apparently satisfying relationships. However, it is not always clear in what way 'good with people' people differ from people who are less skilful. A person who is 'interpersonally competent', as a social psychologist would say, is often described as:

a good listener
able to talk to anyone about anything
not moody, easy to get along with
able to make other people feel at ease
interested in a variety of things, curious about people and inclined to ask lots of questions
having a genuine liking for people
able to get on the right side of people
generally pleasant and agreeable
non-critical
good at organizing people
a good leader

15

Whether these qualities are obvious or appreciated depends on the situation: put two good listeners together and you have a potential social disaster, and the person who *never* criticizes can seem impossibly bland.

However, two rather different sets of qualities emerge from this list. One set has to do with influencing people and getting them to do what you want, and the other with making friends and keeping them. Sometimes these qualities exist in the same person, but more often one set of qualities is present in greater measure than the other. Examples from people we have worked with will help to illustrate this.

James J., an executive at Industrial Chemicals Inc., is good at organizing and directing people, but less good at being liked. An important part of his job is making sure that other people are satisfied and efficient at their jobs. When everyone does as he suggests, and they usually do, his department is highly productive. He does not, however, consider it important that his subordinates like him. As a result, they tend to feel uncomfortable with him and are afraid of his frequent criticisms. If any production problems arise, James responds with increased criticism. His workers are therefore unwilling to discuss things constructively or make suggestions for improvement. James' effectiveness at directing and motivating workers is only useful when things are going smoothly.

On the other hand, Sarah L., an executive in National Investments Ltd, feels that it is important for someone in her position to know her subordinates personally. She often has lunch with them and they tell her about themselves. On several occasions they have told her things about the work situation which she has been able to put right before they became serious. But she finds it difficult to criticize their work. One of her subordinates is ambitious and often volunteers for projects, but is not as capable as some of his colleagues. Once again he volunteers for an important project; despite Sarah's many hints, he doesn't seem to understand that she would rather someone else did it. Nevertheless, she feels unable to give the project to someone else or to insist that it be shared. Her effectiveness at gaining the loyalty and co-operation of her workers is of little use, since she cannot manage and direct their work.

As these examples demonstrate, 'being good with people' is not one single quality. As we are about to show, it is more helpful to think of interpersonal competence as the putting together of a lot of different skills and behaviours. No one skill or behaviour is enough to ensure social success—after all, being able to switch on the ignition does not make one a good driver. Nor will one set of skills see us through every situation; we want different things at different times, even when the situation remains the same. But in every situation we consciously or unconsciously act in ways designed to produce positive rather than negative results. Because no two people go into the same situation with exactly the same goals in mind, it is impossible to say how effective their behaviour is unless we know what they are trying to achieve.

Criteria for social success

Social behaviour can be judged from three different angles. First, does it achieve something concrete (such as getting a book returned, or a social engagement, or increased efficiency)? We call this type of success 'objective effectiveness', since it has to do with whether or not we achieve our objectives in a situation. Second, does it improve the relationships between the people concerned? We call this type of success 'relationship effectiveness', since it has to do with how good we are at improving our relationships with other people. Third, does it make us feel good about ourselves? We call this type of success 'self-respect effectiveness', since it has to do with how well our behaviour manages to enhance our self-esteem and good feelings about ourselves. Every time we come into contact with another person we take a chance in all of these areas. If you try to get your rent reduced, your relationship with your landlord may become rather strained. If you want a friend to do you a favour, you are unlikely to use brutal persuasion, because you know it would damage your friendship. If you back-stab your associates to curry favour with your boss, you are likely to think less of yourself.

So, it is the value each of us places on getting what we want, on being liked, and on keeping our self-respect which determines how we behave, and how satisfying our social encounters are.

But simply being aware of what is important to us in a given situation is not enough. We need to absorb a lot more information before we can pursue our goal with any chance of success.

Who, what and where

Social situations are very complex, even when there are only two people interacting. However, social scientists have developed a number of different ways of analysing social interactions so that useful research can be done. One fairly obvious way of analysing a social situation is to divide it up into Who, What and Where. *Who* are the people involved? *What* is actually taking place between them? *Where* is the interaction taking place? Different sets of conventions and expectations operate in different circumstances, and one must know or at least sense what the rules are in order to function appropriately and effectively. Sometimes the Dos and Don'ts are clearly defined, even written down ('Please fasten your seat belts'). At other times they take the form of 'unwritten rules'.

Who?

Clearly, the relationship between two people dictates what is considered appropriate for each to say or do. This is the Who dimension. One of the strongest influences on any relationship is power, sometimes specified, as in a boss–employee relationship, and sometimes merely 'understood'. Difficulties arise when the parties in an unspecified power relationship fail to agree on who has the power. In a relationship like this the balance of power may be extremely fluid, changing from situation to situation. Take a fairly typical relationship between parents and teenagers. Parents still control many of the material aspects of teenagers' lives, such as pocket-money or use of the family car, but teenage sons and daughters demand considerable freedom of action in the friends and leisure activities they choose. If this power balance is accepted by both sides, all is well, but if it shifts and is not accepted by all concerned, the scene is set for conflict.

The other hugely important element in a relationship is intimacy. We treat lovers, friends and close family very differently from telephone operators and bank clerks. Different sets of rules and expectations apply. There are many other aspects of the Who dimension, which will be discussed in more detail later, but for now we quickly pass on to the What and Where dimensions.

What?

'What' being a somewhat inelegant and unscientific category, the contents of an interaction are usually referred to as an 'agenda'. Examples of agendas include selling, buying, bargaining, persuading, resisting persuasion, playing games, enjoying oneself, and so on. If two people have the same agenda, then co-operation will be an appropriate behaviour, but if their agendas are diametrically opposed (one wants to take a vacation and the other is too busy to take a vacation) then some arguing, or persuasion, is almost inevitable. Of course, if we assume we know what the other person's agenda is, and are wrong, the chances of our behaviour being effective are fairly small.

Where?

In the course of a day we have many different agendas with people with whom we have a variety of relationships, and our behaviour always reflects the subtle interaction between agenda and relationship— almost certainly we would use different words to say 'no' to a persistent salesperson and 'no' to a close friend. But if we take account of a third element, the Where of an interaction, this picture becomes subtler still. We meet and talk and work with other people in many different settings, or arenas. A restaurant is a setting, so is a theatre, a sports field, an accounts department, a boardroom, a court of law, and all of them have their conventions. Very few people would dream of humming loudly to themselves in the witness box or telling the waiter to sit down and enjoy the party.

Many of the settings we are required to operate in are so large and tightly structured that we have little chance of influencing them. Into this category come governments, public service companies, big corporations, tax authorities, banks and the legal system. Their conventions are highly visible and usually inflexible, and expressed as laws, policies and statutes. Smaller settings tend to have looser structures and fewer rules, although the latter may be every bit as binding as an Act of Congress or Parliament. Many esoteric clubs, for example, have extraordinary, even ridiculous, rules and customs.

The power factor

The mix of skills needed to work effectively with or within a large organization is, generally speaking, rather different from that required in relation to smaller settings. In many instances, it is the big organization which offers the greatest material rewards. We are back to 'power' again. By virtue of their size, big organizations wield great power, often with considerable power discrepancies existing between the 'roles' and 'castes' within them. Company chairmen obviously have more power than secretaries, teachers more than pupils, archbishops more than curates. Politics and social change are power struggles. The providers of vital services and commodities (air-traffic controllers, sewage workers, miners, the members of OPEC) are wielders of power.

Research, for example that by Michener and Suchner in the early 1970s, only confirms what most of us have suspected: that powerful people, people who can reward or punish, behave differently than do people who seek to be rewarded or not punished.

21

High-power people talk more frequently and direct their communication primarily to other high-power people, whereas low-power individuals also direct conversation toward high-power people.

An interesting study by Ronald Lippitt and associates was conducted at a boys' summer camp in Wisconsin to see if high-power children behaved differently from low-power children. The children in four camp cabins were individually shown pictures of each member of their cabin and asked to rank them in order of power on a series of nails tacked to the cabin wall. The definition of power given to the children was 'who is best at getting others to do what he wants them to do'. This exercise was completed during the first week of camp and, for the rest of the four-week session, observations were made of each of the children's behaviour with respect to the others.

In general, the findings were that more powerful children make more frequent attempts to influence the behaviour of others and are more successful in these attempts. The more powerful children were more direct in their influence attempts (more likely to order the other boys to do something), whereas the less powerful boys were more likely to act submissively and to respond deferentially to the high-power children. The power these boys wielded was unrelated to their height, weight, and overall activity level and only slightly related to intelligence, with the brighter children somewhat more likely to be seen as powerful.

Boys rated as particularly low in power were observed to be less often socially involved with other children; the low-power children tended to be either very little involved in camp activities and the use of camp equipment or else they were involved in non-social activities to a very great extent. High-power children were highly social (talking, playing with others) and only moderately interested in camp activities that did not include socializing. When children were asked to rank themselves in the power hierarchy, they tended to be accurate in their ratings:

they rated themselves as did the others in their cabin.

For these children, as for us, the role in which we find ourselves often dictates the kind of behaviour we can use most effectively, as well as the kind of behaviour we are likely to choose. Our goals in large, well-structured arenas may well be limited by our place in the hierarchy, however we may have come to that place. In the above study, it is not clear whether the children with high power achieved that by virtue of their confident behaviour and 'bossy' ways or whether they became confident and assertive as a result of their experiences. A camp is a relatively unstructured arena, unlike many of the situations in which adults find themselves. A secretary sits in an open reception area, an executive behind a closed door in a private office. Obviously, it is not their current behaviour that is responsible for the power differential.

If organizations provide us with money, status, careers, and essential services, individual people provide us with other things, and our goals in personal relationships are rather different.

Person to person

Most of our personal relationships involve a small number of people whom we know quite well, or would like to know well, and most of the time our expectations of such people are not stated directly — we would probably not approach a new acquaintance and say, 'I want to be your friend.' Instead, we behave in ways (issuing invitations, doing small favours) which we hope will bring about a state of friendship. Conversely, expectations in the personal arena, although unspecified, may be quite rigid and inflexible. In fact relationships often end because one or other of these unwritten laws is broken: for example, something told in confidence is repeated to a third

23

person. Techniques which increase relationship effectiveness (see Chapter 6) are often the most useful in person-to-person arenas. The goal of an interaction between two people, whether they are sexual intimates, friends, classmates, workmates or members of the same family, may be the gaining of some concrete objective, but usually the maintenance of the relationship has high priority.

Social skills

We often use the phrase 'good at' to refer to someone who shows a set of skilled behaviours: she is a good (skilled) driver, he is a good (skilled) tennis player. There is, however, a certain resistance to using the word 'skilled' when we talk about being good with people. Instead, we use words like 'friendly' or 'sociable'. This is probably because we like to think of social interactions as being 'natural' and 'spontaneous'. To a certain extent they are, but this is only because the skills involved have been so well learned that we are able to perform them without thinking. The impromptu jam sessions of jazz musicians, for example, are only possible because each of them is a highly skilled instrumentalist. Once we have learned to drive a car, or to swim, or even to tie our shoelaces, we forget the laborious hours of practice it took to reach that level of skill. This 'practice' is so much a part of growing up that we are never aware of it happening and therefore underestimate the amount of learning that went into producing an apparently 'natural' performance.

The idea that social interactions are spontaneous is therefore true up to a point, but not very helpful to people who want to change aspects of their social behaviour. There can be few of us who have not tried to 'plan' a social encounter, such as seeking a raise or asking for a date, or conducted post-mortems with ourselves when things did not turn out quite as we would have liked. One of the aims of this book is to help the reader become more effective with people, using goals, relationships, agendas and arenas as a framework for analysing both situations and behaviour.

How are social skills acquired?

If we accept that effective social behaviour is a complex set of skills, then we can assume that the principles of learning which govern the acquisition of skilled behaviour in general will apply here. These principles will be discussed more fully in later chapters but, briefly, any skill is learned by breaking it up into manageable units or 'sub-skills' first (few of us would take a second lesson from a driving instructor who simply said 'Drive'), and by practising and being rewarded for performing these sub-units successfully (when we press the accelerator in the correct manner

the car goes forward smoothly). Only when all of these sub-units are put together and repeated many times do we produce what seems like a spontaneous performance.

A good example of these principles applied to the teaching of assertive behaviour is provided by research carried out by the first author of this book and Marvin and Anita Goldfried. In this study we developed long lists of very specific actions and ways of thinking which we thought would work in situations requiring assertive behaviour (standing up for one's views, being honest about what one wants). We then asked our research volunteers to focus on these, practise them in imaginary situations and eventually practise them in real life. At first this role-playing, where our volunteers had to focus very consciously on their own thoughts and behaviour, seemed very artificial and often got in the way of their performance. As training progressed, however, the desired responses became more learned, and with time required less and less attention and thought. We found that clients receiving this training greatly improved their assertion skills in real-life situations. These results suggest that paying attention to what one is doing and consciously focusing on the particular skills needed will eventually lead to greater effectiveness. There are now a great many studies which have produced similar findings and which point to the conclusion that people can be helped, or can help themselves, to change their social behaviour if they go about it systematically.

2

Thinking, feeling, acting and learning

Tenterhooks are the upholstery of the anxious seat.

ROBERT SHERWOOD (1896–1955)

In order to understand what skills are needed for effective social behaviour and how to make the most of them, we first need to understand some general principles of social behaviour *per se*, regardless of how successful it is. We will begin by describing a general system which psychologists have found useful for categorizing many sorts of behaviour, including social behaviour.

Behaviour

To begin at the beginning, we need to define just what we mean by the term 'behaviour'. Behaviour refers to any of a person's activities which can be observed or measured. Today psychologists can not only observe and measure what we do, but also, indirectly, what we think and feel. To a behavioural psychologist the layman's definition of behaviour is only one aspect, the obvious and visible aspect, of behaviour—in

psychological terminology that is *overt behaviour*. The other aspects of behaviour, not generally thought of as behaviour by the lay person, are *cognitive behaviour* and *physiological behaviour*, or thinking and feeling. All three aspects of behaviour are involved in most social encounters. As we will see later, each of them forms an important part of overall social skill.

Inside your head

Cognitive behaviours include not only thinking but all our 'mental' behaviours. In general, the ways in which we obtain and use information and knowledge can be thought of as cognitive behaviours. Although we do not usually think of memory or sight as behaviours, cognitive psychologists now believe that these processes are actually things that people *do* and, as such, can be thought of as behaviours. One theory, for example, claims that our perceptions of the world, based on our sense of sight, hearing, smell, taste and touch, are active explorations of our environment. We are selective in the information we pick up (why else should the world seem to be full of advertisements for food when we are dieting?) and actively combine and compare this with information we already hold. Even such processes as memory are now viewed as the capacity actively to reconstruct particular events or sense impressions. Memory is something we *do*, not something we *have*. Since it is possible to measure whether a person remembers something or not, memory can fairly be categorized as a cognitive behaviour.

There are, of course, many other cognitive behaviours besides taking note of our environment and remembering. These include channelling our attention, making decisions, thinking, and solving problems. As we will show, each of these plays an important role in our ability to interact successfully with other people.

Physiology: body processes

Physiological activities include all our internal biological reactions and life processes, such as heart-rate, blood pressure, stomach contractions, blushing and so on. As with cognitive processes, we are not often used to hearing bodily processes labelled as behaviour. This is because we usually think of 'behaviour' as something under our own control. We assume that body metabolism isn't—it simply happens. But when we talk of people 'working themselves into a rage' or trying to 'keep calm' we are, in fact, talking of controlling physiological responses, and there are many studies which show that this is perfectly possible. A number of researchers have demonstrated that people can be taught to increase and decrease their heart rate. Investigators at Harvard University have repeatedly demonstrated that people can learn to raise and lower their blood pressure; the second author of this book has had a long involvement with a biofeedback treatment programme designed to lower the blood pressure of hypertensive patients. Edward

Blanchard and Leonard Epstein, reviewing biofeed-back methods as a whole, have concluded that they can enable people to lower their body temperature voluntarily, control the acid level in their stomach, regulate muscle tension, modify electrical activity in the brain, and even improve eyesight by altering the curvature of the eye.

Though we may not be aware of physiological activities most of the time, they are detectable by sophisticated measuring instruments (electrocardio-graph, electroencephalograph, etc.). Other body events can quite easily be felt and controlled simply by paying attention to them. If you focus on tense muscles, for example, you can usually relax them at least momentarily. Relaxation is one of the standard techniques of reducing anxiety (see page 133).

Emotions are included in the physiological beha-viour category, because they cannot exist without a physiological response. This response is often our only means of knowing that someone is in the grip of emotion—the person may be shaking with fear (or is it rage?) or blushing with embarrassment. Without some sort of physical response, we would not say that a person was experiencing an emotion. But the fact that the same physiological state appears to underlie a whole variety of emotions shows that we must be sensitive to non-physiological cues when trying to interpret other people's emotions.

Our emotional responses to other people and theirs to us make an important contribution to the quality and effectiveness of our interactions. The expression 'I was so angry/anxious/upset/shy/embarrassed I couldn't think straight' illustrates that at times our emotions are so intense that they seriously interfere with the way we would like to behave. At other times, we have to work hard at generating enough energy or motivation to interact with people at all. The rela-tionship of emotions to physiological activities sug-gests that the better we are at controlling our bodily responses, the better we will be at controlling our emotions in time of need.

What others see

The 'overt behaviour' category includes all the activities we are most used to thinking of as behaviour, all the things we do which are readily observable without instruments—sitting, walking, talking, gesturing and so on. Students of social behaviour also find it useful to divide overt behaviour into two categories, verbal and non-verbal. Verbal behaviours include not only what people say but how they say it. Examples of non-verbal behaviour are body posture (whether we stand or sit upright, slouched, legs together or apart or crossed, arms folded across the body or relaxed by our sides), facial expression, physical distance or closeness, touching, clothes, cosmetics, ornaments . . .

Non-verbal behaviour is fascinating for many reasons. We seem, for example, to pay much more attention to it than to verbal behaviour when we make judgements about other people. Also, although we

Is this non-verbal LANGUAGE?

use non-verbal cues to make these judgements, we are often quite unable to pinpoint exactly which cues these are: they register with us powerfully but unconsciously. Nor is non-verbal behaviour as easy to control as verbal behaviour: we often rehearse or censor what we say but our non-verbal performance is not so controllable, it tends to 'give us away'. People who are asked to lie, for example, can be relied on to show tell-tale non-verbal behaviours such as foot shuffling, avoiding eye gaze or covering the mouth with the hand. No wonder psychologists talk of 'non-verbal leakage'!

The total picture

Categorizing behaviour as we have just done is more than an interesting intellectual exercise. Many social conflicts are, in fact, the result of assuming that all three categories always go together. Certainly, there are occasions when we think, feel and act simultaneously. Imagine a little girl who has just trodden mud into the house for the fourth time in one afternoon. Seemingly, all at once, her mother thinks 'Not again! I told her to wipe her feet' (cognitive behaviour), feels her face flushing, her heart pounding, and herself become very angry (physiological behaviour), and yells at her daughter (overt behaviour). But there are times when behaviour in one category does not match or occur at the same time as that in another.

Joe W. might think his boss's idea for an advertising campaign is lousy, but he says just the opposite. Or we stop ourselves paying a compliment or asking for a date because we are afraid of the outcome. Or we decide that our overt behaviour should override our gut reaction—many air passengers are a little scared of flying, but fly nonetheless. Indeed, if we never pursued one category of behaviour at the expense of the others, we would be very difficult to live with and sometimes totally inactive. Imagine a person who always blurted out their every thought—they would have some difficulty making or keeping friends; or a person who never approached situations they were afraid of—they would be in a permanent state of suspended animation.

We readily accept that thinking, feeling and doing do not necessarily go together in ourselves, because we know what we are thinking, feeling and doing. When we look at others, however, all we can know (unless they choose to tell us) is what they *do*. If someone apparently snubs us at a party, we might assume that it is deliberate—they did not want to talk to us—but it might equally be that they feel shy, or have not seen us, or were about to come over when we turned away to talk to someone else. Social psychologists have demonstrated just how often we make mistakes in interpreting other people's behaviour, because all we can see is their overt behaviour. It seems that we are more likely to explain other people's behaviour in terms of personal traits such as shyness, hostility, irritability and so on than in terms of environmental factors, such as being in the wrong place at the wrong time. It was thought that this difference might be because we lack certain vital information, but it seems that even when good information is available we often ignore it. In one 'quiz' experiment, subjects were randomly assigned the role of 'contestant' or 'quizmaster'; the quizmaster was asked to devise his own questions and to make them as difficult and esoteric as possible. Students who watched the 'quiz' always rated the contestant as less able than the quizmaster, even though they knew how the quiz was set up, with all the advantages stacked on the quizmaster's side.

When and how behaviours in these different categories—thinking, feeling and doing—go together is the outcome of learning patterns in particular situations. One child might be punished for fighting when angry, whereas another might be praised—one learns to bottle up angry feelings, the other that feeling angry and hitting out go together. Some children are taught to keep a 'stiff upper lip' when they are afraid, and to act unafraid in situations they want to avoid—again a particular feeling (fear) and a particular action (acting unafraid) become strongly linked. On the other hand, a child who learns that showing fear always brings other people to the rescue will link the same feeling (fear) with the opposite action (acting afraid). In certain situations, we all learn to act counter to our thoughts or feelings. We learn to say thank you for gifts we like and dislike and to tell others they look nice even if we think they don't.

Part of the 'social sensitivity' we will be discussing in later chapters involves being aware of possible mismatches in the three categories and taking these into account when interpreting other people's behaviour.

The learning process

Almost all human behaviour, including social behaviour, can be seen as the outcome of (a) the situation in which the behaviour occurs, and (b) past experience of the same or similar situations . . . which is really the same as saying that as the situation changes, so does our behaviour. We yell and scream at football matches, but are subdued and silent at funerals. We relax and talk easily and frankly with close friends, but are alert and guarded with a new boss. We also tend to behave rather differently in one-to-one situations and group situations. Our behaviour with our children is probably quite different from our behaviour with people of our own age, or old people, or the disabled, or foreigners.

Just as variations in our environment, including the physical 'scenery' and the people in it, produce variations in our behaviour, changes in our behaviour often have a marked effect on our environments, especially on the people in them. The two are inextricably linked—behaviour influences environment, and environment behaviour.

The truth of this can be seen by asking—if environment determines behaviour, why doesn't everyone act the same in similar situations? The answer is that individual behaviour in a given environment is determined by that person's prior experience of the same, or similar, situations. If people have different learning experiences, they will behave differently. These learning-based differences in behaviour are at their most noticeable in the area of social behaviour, where radically different cultures provide very different learning experiences for their members. One person, an Italian, say, learns to express emotions freely in front of others, laughing, crying, becoming visibly angry; another person, an Englishman, perhaps, learns to keep his emotions to himself.

That does not mean to say there are not many differences within the same culture. No two people react identically in identical situations, because their learning experiences are different. These experiences, of course, continue throughout life, so to understand why someone does something in the present, we must know something about their past and also about their current learning experiences. Admittedly, familiarity with someone's life history is difficult in the early stages of a relationship! Indeed, etiquette dictates that we do *not* reveal too much of our own history or display too much curiosity about other people's until a later stage in the relationship. However, never forget that in any interaction *you* form part of the other person's current learning experience. If your behaviour towards them is similar to that of other people, you are replicating their earlier experiences and strengthening their tendency to act in the way they do. So, if you ignore someone who is unfriendly, they are likely to continue behaving in an unfriendly manner. Conversely, if you are friendly towards them, you are giving them a different learning experience which, if it continues for long enough, will change their behaviour. In a similar way you can change your own behaviour by creating new learning experiences for yourself. When we talk of 'getting out of a rut' or of 'trying to meet new people', we are doing just that.

Psychologists studying how learning experiences and environments come to change our behaviour have identified three major types of learning: (a) effect learning, (b) associative learning and (c) observational learning. These are the three pillars of *social learning theory*, the theory which says that the social lessons we learn are dinned into us by the social consequences of our behaviour. Since to a large extent social effectiveness depends on understanding not only why we and others act as we do, but also how to bring about change, it is worth saying a little more about these three types of social learning.

Learning by results

There has been an enormous amount of psychological research on how the effects of past behaviour govern future behaviour. The first person to formulate this relationship was Edward Thorndike, who in 1898 published the results of a number of laboratory studies done on animals. Thorndike proved that the effects of past behaviour strongly influence current behaviour. He called this relationship the Law of Effect. By far the most prodigious investigator of the learning principles underlying the Law of Effect has been B. F. Skinner, the well-known Harvard psychologist, who has contributed in this area for over 40 years. Many of the ideas presented here about increasing the positive effects of interpersonal relationships are based on the principles discovered by Skinner and his colleagues.

Much of our behaviour, including most of our interpersonal behaviour, is governed by, or in some way related to, its consequences or effects. We try a new recipe; if it turns out well we use it again, and if it doesn't we don't. If we sound pleased when someone telephones, they are more likely to call again than if we sound bored or in a hurry to put the receiver down.

Any behaviour can have three types of effect:

positive, negative or neutral. Behaviour followed by positive effects is likely to be repeated and strengthened in future similar situations. This process is called reinforcement. If what we do produces a negative effect in a particular setting, we are less likely to do the same thing again, or at least not in the same type of situation. Neutral effects, neither good nor bad, have little effect on behaviour.

There are several reasons why a knowledge of effect learning is crucial if we want to change our social behaviour. First, it can prompt us to find out what is reinforcing or punishing for other people and to try to provide or avoid it. There is nothing artificial about this process—we all do it consciously from time to time when we try to please someone we like. The person who says 'Take me as you find me' is likely to find that, after a while, no one takes them.

Second, it helps to bear in mind that our behaviour in social interactions is always a consequence or effect to someone else. Although we may not be aware of it, we often subtly punish the people we interact with—by not listening properly, for example, or turning away when they are talking to us, or talking too much about ourselves. Unless we provide positive effects for the people we mix with, their 'approach behaviour' (to use the terminology of learning theorists) will be weakened or, in everyday language, they will not want to be friendly.

Finally, we must know what we ourselves find rewarding or punishing (do we really want to go to a party or would we rather read a book?), otherwise we will continually find ourselves in situations where it is difficult to be effective.

All these processes are discussed in greater detail in Chapter 6.

Learning by association

Have you ever found yourself transported back to childhood by a particular smell, or noticed that your mood improves or worsens by being in a certain place? Associative learning principles explain how such reactions come about. The process is quite simple. If a neutral event is associated with an event which automatically produces a response, then very soon the automatic reaction becomes the natural reaction to the neutral event. This type of learning is especially important in the learning of emotional responses. When we talk of objects having 'sentimental value' we are describing just this process: objects with little intrinsic worth—theatre programmes, birthday cards—are highly valued because of their association with some positive event or person, and even years later can arouse the same pleasant emotions.

Understanding associative learning can be an important means of increasing social effectiveness, and in several ways. If our presence or absence is associated in people's minds with very pleasant or unpleasant events, they come to respond to us in the way they responded to the events themselves. We have all, on occasion, tried to avoid someone who has seen us in an embarrassing situation; similarly, we come to associate people who are generous with praise or criticism with the feelings which praise and criticism produce.

Associative learning of emotional responses can therefore be very important in relationships. It can also be important in objective effectiveness, for getting what we want, if our objective is somehow tied up with another person's emotional responses. In addition, our learned responses to our *own* behaviour can determine whether we behave in ways which maintain or damage our self-respect: behaviour which we associate with negative events is likely to set off feelings of guilt or anxiety. To some extent, most of us base our self-respect on how we feel about our own behaviour.

Learning by observation

Although learning by results and by association are extremely important parts of the learning process, both depend on direct, first-hand experience of the environment. Nevertheless, some researchers have proposed that much of the complex behaviour we learn, and particularly behaviour we learn rapidly, depends not on direct experience but on observation and imitation. It is difficult to overestimate the importance of these two processes—the first stages in the learning of any skill are usually based on them, as are the fashion and advertising industries! Deaf children do not learn to talk without specialized teaching because they cannot hear (observe) or imitate sounds. At times we are acutely conscious of learning through imitation (we watch to see which knife and fork our host picks up first); at others, the process is entirely unconscious (we take on the accent or speech habits of those around us).

By observing other people we not only learn new behaviours, but also their likely consequences. Every day advertisers suggest that all sorts of wonderful consequences will follow from using Brand X—they are relying on just this process of vicarious learning.

Learning by observation also includes learning about things by listening and reading.

It is not difficult to imagine the effect of many, or immensely few, opportunities for observation and imitation on learning. People who are socially effective often have parents who were good with people and exposed them to a variety of social situations. The reverse is also true: many people who seek to change their social behaviour say that their parents were shy and that they seldom saw them mixing successfully with others. To some extent, later reading and observation can remedy this lack of learning opportunities. Indeed, every interaction every day can be thought of as an opportunity for learning.

3

What stops us being socially effective?

Men are polished, through act and speech,
    each by each,
As the pebbles are smoothed on the
    rolling beach.

J. T. TROWBRIDGE (1827–1916)

If one counts all the separate skills which go into being socially effective, one begins to wonder how anyone ever learns all of them. Many people, however, seem to manage it—at least some of the time. As we saw in the last chapter, most social skills are learned through our experiences with the environment and the people in it.

A long apprenticeship

One reason why most people seem to learn at least some of the necessary skills is that *Homo sapiens* has a very long process of socialization—most of us live in families or some other structured setting for the first 13 to 18 years of our lives. During this social apprenticeship, we are expected to master an increasing range of social skills. Young children learn (often with some difficulty) to be generally 'nice' to people by saying 'please' and 'thank you' and refraining from unkind remarks. They also learn to co-operate through play. However, they are not expected to possess more than rudimentary conversation skills. Lapses from social grace are tolerated and even considered funny in a way that most certainly would not be in an adult.

TRY saying, 'GET LOST', nicely...

Adolescents, as well as mastering the niceties of 'manners', and expanding their general conversation skills and ability to function away from the family, must begin to learn the complex skills of relating to the opposite sex—'chatting up', asking for dates and refusing unwanted advances. And a few years after that they are thrown into and expected to cope with a vast range of social situations each requiring slightly different skills. Given the complexity of the adult social repertoire, it is hardly surprising that few people are expert across all situations.

Because so much of the unhappiness which therapists see among their clients originates in problems in interacting with others, psychologists have worked hard to try to account for deficiencies in social skills, and to suggest ways of remedying them.

Most of the theories proposed come under one of three headings: (a) the skill deficit model, (b) the response inhibition model and (c) the choice model. No one of these adequately explains all of a person's social ineffectiveness. Rather, each is useful in explaining some cases and all three must be taken together to give a complete explanation of why it is that all of us some of the time and some of us much of the time find it difficult to interact effectively.

Skill deficit model

This model assumes that people are ineffective because they do not have or 'know' the appropriate social behaviour in a particular situation. The deficit may be quite specific—not knowing how to refuse requests for favours—or more general—never listening or being unable to initiate conversations. Obviously a person with the second, more general kind of deficit will have the greater handicap, the skills they lack being necessary across a wider range of situations.

Because the greater part of teaching social skills takes place in childhood, it follows that parents who are themselves deficient in certain skills, or over-protective, will be inadequate teachers. Also if a child is an only child or has few playmates she or he will be deprived of many opportunities for observational learning. One review of a number of child studies concluded that children who lack social skills are more likely to develop into delinquents or need psychiatric help than children socially competent for their age.

It is very unfortunate that after childhood, and even during it, the teaching of social skills is such a hit-and-miss affair. While responsible parents usually do their best to instil acceptable social habits into their children (share your toys, don't stare, use your handkerchief, tell Grandma about school), as adolescents and adults we are more or less on our own. The adolescent who does not seem to be 'making it' with girls rarely approaches his more successful peers and asks them what *they* do. And even if he did, they might not be able to tell him. Still less is he going to ask the girls who reject him what he is doing wrong.

Pinpointing the deficit

It is all very well to tell someone to stop criticizing us, but we never tell them how to change our behaviour by more constructive means. We don't tell someone who is boring us how they could make their conversation more interesting—we simply avoid them. Certainly, people who are ineffective are usually aware that they are doing *something* wrong. The problem is to obtain more specific and more constructive feedback. Part of the difficulty is that we cannot see or hear ourselves as others see and hear us—people who hear themselves on tape or see themselves on video for the first time are usually amazed. Most of the time we are quite unaware of our gestures and ways of talking. Try to keep track of your eye-gaze or your facial expression or the intonation of your voice during one brief social interaction and you will quickly see what we mean!

Given these difficulties and the haphazard nature of the learning process, it is hardly surprising that most of us have some social skill gaps. Nevertheless, there are personal factors which can make the learning process even more difficult, partly because they alter the way in which people react to us, and partly because they influence the speed and efficiency of our learning. These include sex, physical appearance and disorders such as autism, mental handicap and hyperactivity.

Masculine and feminine

As well as learning general social skills, men and women must learn those skills which our culture deems appropriate for their sex. Research has confirmed that women are, in general, more eager to please—in dress, speech and attitudes—than men. Men, again in general, operate on a more 'take me or leave me' basis. One experiment showed that it was impossible to find any occupation where women were expected to be more effective than men. That was in the United States, but much the same picture emerges elsewhere. Since we know from various other studies that people tend to conform to the expectations others have of them, it is conceivable that women learn to be less effective than men in certain social situations. In dating and courtship, society certainly expects men to display a different set of skills from women. One effect of the blurring of sex roles we are now seeing is that the majority of men say they have no idea how to refuse unwanted advances politely or accept them graciously, and women that they do not know how to pay restaurant bills, make direct requests for dates or relate to male work colleagues.

Physical appearance

If you ask someone what they like or dislike about a person, probably the last reason they will come up with is attractiveness or plainness. And yet there is a substantial body of research showing that appearance is one of the most important determinants of our initial reaction to a person. Attractive people are seen by others not only as happier and more successful, but as having more socially desirable personality traits. Among the middle-aged, an attractive person is judged to be of higher status, more socially outgoing and more pleasant than a plain person. Even amongst children, popularity is related to attractiveness. What is interesting about these findings is that they are equally true for judgements of the same and the opposite sex. If some people automatically elicit positive responses from others, the principles of effect learning predict that they should become generally more skilful than people who tend to elicit negative responses.

Fortunately, our appearance is highly modifiable—we can change our wardrobe, wear ornaments, lose or gain weight, even have plastic surgery. There are of course limits to the physical and outward changes we can make, but that should not render us helpless in the face of negative judgements. Ray Bull and Julia Stevens of North East London Polytechnic conducted a number of studies into people's reactions to disfigurement, and found that most of us tend to stand further away from disfigured people and to look at them less often during conversation. On the other hand, they also found that the behaviour of the disfigured person was very important: if he or she behaved in a friendly manner—smiling, making eye contact occasionally, displaying interest in the other person—then this initial negative reaction lessened. So we can say, with a great deal of confidence, that appearances are not everything. They do indeed have a strong effect on people's reactions to us on first meeting or on casual acquaintance, but the ultimate success of our relationships depends on how we behave.

Autism, mental handicap and hyperactivity

These are disorders which hamper social effective-ness, because they hamper the learning of social skills. Autistic children, for example, appear to be unresponsive to social cues—parents usually report that such children are 'different' from birth. There are four general characteristics which define autism: the child reacts as if other people do not exist and fails to develop interpersonal behaviour, there is an absence or distortion of language, the child is preoccupied with sameness, and, finally, medical examinations reveal no gross neurological impairment.

Children who are mentally handicapped, on the other hand, are often very responsive to others, but their limited learning capacity may make it difficult for them to acquire complex social skills. It is not that they are unable to learn, but that they need more intensive teaching. Unfortunately, many parents underestimate a handicapped child's learning capacity or imagine that he or she will never need certain skills, such as travelling alone or relating to the opposite sex, and therefore make no attempt to teach them. In general, however, there is very little relationship between intelligence and social effectiveness. Being clever certainly does not guarantee social success.

Children described as hyperactive are just that: they consistently display high levels of activity in situations where it is clearly inappropriate. They rarely inhibit this activity on command, and often seem capable of only one speed of responding. These behaviour patterns interfere with learning. Either the child does not register or pay attention to the information necessary for successful social interaction, or becomes so frustrating and unrewarding for other people that they give up trying to teach social behaviours.

A number of other disorders, such as blindness, deafness or physical handicap, can also interfere with the learning of social skills, but not inevitably. The provision of more structured and more intensive learning environments can help to overcome such disadvantages.

The skill deficit model, therefore, assumes that there are characteristics in the person and / or the environment which get in the way of learning effective social behaviour. Almost all psychotherapy is designed, in one way or another, to provide new and better learning experiences so that such deficits can be gradually overcome. And not only professional therapists can give this sort of help. Sympathetic and socially skilled friends can be invaluable (and in any case will have their own deficits which *you* may be able to remedy). Each time we talk with friends about social behaviour, observe or read about people with good social skills, or reflect carefully on our own behaviour and its effects on others, we open the door to learning new skills.

Response inhibition model

Even if we *do* succeed in learning social skills during our childhood and adolescence, this does not guarantee that we will be able to use them at will. The response inhibition model suggests that we often bottle up, distort, or over-ride effective responses and that these inhibitions have three main sources: high emotional arousal, or being out of control emotionally, unrealistic or unreasonable beliefs or expectations, and automatic behaviour which somehow 'slips out' before we have a chance to act in a more appropriate way (the I've-put-my-foot-in-it-again feeling).

When emotions interfere

One of the most potent inhibitors of behaviour in any context is the emotion of anxiety. We have all experienced situations where we are so tensed up that it is impossible to apply our skills effectively. All too often this happens at times when we particularly want to do well or when we do not have a set of automatic or well-rehearsed things to do and say—interviews for important jobs, first dates, even appearances on television. A common source of anxiety in these situations is the knowledge that we lack some, but not all, of the necessary skills—we may be a good listener but a mediocre conversationalist. Unfortunately, thinking about our shortcomings often disrupts the skills we have. This is why skill deficit and response inhibition so often go hand in hand.

John S. is a newly divorced 41-year-old man who is interested in getting to know some single women. Although he has never had difficulty making conversation with people, he has known for a long time that he does not know how to initiate an interaction with a woman he has never met (skill deficit). When he goes to a party to meet people, he is acutely aware of his inability to use the kind of small talk necessary to open a conversation. He stands miserably against the wall, watching others and feeling more and more inadequate. When a woman does begin to talk to him, he finds himself so anxious that he is unable to carry on his end of the conversation (response inhibition), even though he is quite capable of maintaining a conversation under less trying circumstances.

Beliefs which sabotage

Just about any error in our interpretation of what is currently happening or in our predictions of what might happen, can interfere with effective behaviour. As the following case history shows, faulty interpretations and predictions can play havoc with every aspect of effectiveness.

Susan S. was a client in one of our therapy studies, and quite effective in most social situations except when it came to saying No. She knew *how* to do it and could identify in the abstract *when* saying no was appropriate but when faced with the actual situation she froze and said Yes instead of No. If we could have peeped into her mind in one of these situations, we would have found these thoughts racing through it: 'I can't refuse to do that. What if she can't get anyone else? She'll think I'm awful for saying no and I'll look selfish, as if I only do things for myself. She won't like me!' Needless to say, thoughts such as these make refusing very difficult—they would stop almost anyone from saying No.

Still on the subject of unrealistic or unreasonable beliefs, two American researchers found very few overt behavioural differences between men who went out with lots of women and men who went out with very few, but what they did find was that the 'low daters' had a correspondingly low opinion of themselves. Presumably they dated infrequently because they assumed that women would not want to go out with them, or that they would be rejected after one date.

REALITY?
What's reality
ever done for me?

Seeing the world through the wrong window

Aaron Beck, an American psychiatrist who works with very depressed people, has suggested that behind most ineffective behaviour, and depression in particular, lie a number of distorted thought processes. Arbitrary inference, the drawing of a conclusion when evidence is lacking or is actually contrary to it (for example, believing that people will not like you if you ask for a favour), and magnification or exaggeration of the meaning of an event (assuming that your boss's refusal to give you a raise means that your hard work is not appreciated) are two examples of the cognitive styles which Beck believes can inhibit effectiveness. Obviously if you believe, incorrectly, that asking for favours will cause people to dislike you, you will be reluctant to ask for the things you need or deserve, and so be obliged to sacrifice objectives which are very important to you. If your job is important to you and you believe (wrongly) that you are under-appreciated and underpaid, you are likely to get extremely frustrated, perhaps to the point of quitting—which achieves nothing.

Albert Ellis, a New York psychologist and psycho-therapist, has also suggested that ineffective social behaviour, and much emotional distress, is a result of faulty beliefs and irrational ideas. According to Ellis, typical irrational beliefs are:

1 The idea that it is a dire necessity for an adult human being to be loved or approved by virtually every significant other person in the community.

2 The idea that one should be thoroughly competent, adequate, and achieving in all possible respects, if one is to consider oneself worthwhile.

3 The idea that certain people are bad, wicked or villainous and that they should be severely blamed and punished for their villainy.

4 The idea that it is awful and catastrophic when things are not the way one would very much like them to be.

5 The idea that human unhappiness is externally caused and that people have little or no ability to control their sorrows and disturbances.

6 The idea that if something is or may be dangerous or fearsome one should be terribly concerned about it and should keep dwelling on the possibility of its occurring.

7 The idea that it is easier to avoid than to face certain life difficulties and self-responsibilities.

8 The idea that one should be dependent on others and need someone stronger than oneself on whom to rely.

9 The idea that one's past history is an all-important determinant of one's present behaviour and that because something once strongly affected one's life, it should have a similar effect indefinitely.

10 The idea that one should become quite upset over other people's problems and disturbances.

11 The idea that there is invariably a right, precise, and perfect solution to human problems and that it is catastrophic if this correct solution is not found.

'Catastrophizing'

It is not so much a question of actually believing these things as behaving *as if* we did. When we get very angry or upset at things not going our way, we are behaving as if we believed the whole world is against us—we are 'catastrophizing'. When we become very depressed at being ignored or rejected, we are saying, in effect, 'I am entitled to the love and attention of the whole world', which is patently unreasonable. Ellis's list is a very good scale against which to measure one's expectations of the world—indeed, most people find it very revealing.

The following dialogue is a brief example of how a therapist might deal with a few unrealistic expectations and beliefs a client appears to have about his relationship with his wife:

THERAPIST How have things been going with you and your family?

CLIENT Not at all well—that's why I have to come to therapy. If I got support from people, I wouldn't need to pay somebody to help me.

THERAPIST What kind of support would you like that you are not getting now?

CLIENT Well, for one thing, my wife doesn't listen to me like she used to before she got this job. She doesn't care about me the way she used to—it's as if the job is more important than me. That really scares me—I don't know what I'll do if she leaves me.

THERAPIST You've just mentioned a number of different issues: you think your wife's behaviour has changed since she started her job; you interpret this as meaning that she doesn't care as much about you as she used to; you are concerned that she might consider her job as more important than she considers you; and, finally, you are afraid that she might leave you and that, if she does, it will be awful for you. Does that seem to sum it up?

CLIENT Yes. Isn't that enough?

THERAPIST That is a lot of worry for you to be carrying around. Let's start with the beginning of this sequence of worries: that which started you thinking that she might leave you. You noticed that your wife doesn't listen to you as much as she did before she got the job. Have you mentioned this to her?

CLIENT No, I just try talking to her and she's always rushing off to do the washing or handle one of the kids or something—anything is more important than I am.

THERAPIST It sounds as if one of your underlying assumptions is that if your wife attends to jobs around the house (or around the office), she is proving to you that those things are more important to her than you are. Does that describe how you feel?

CLIENT Yes.

THERAPIST Why haven't you told your wife that you would like to talk to her more?

CLIENT Well, I feel she can *see* that I want to talk, but she deliberately chooses to do other things. If she really cared about me, she would want to talk to me as much as I want to talk to her—also, if she cared, she would see how unhappy I am and ask me about it. I'd be delighted to tell her then.

THERAPIST It sounds as if another of your underlying beliefs is that if your wife cared about you, she would notice that you are unhappy and she would ask you what was wrong.

CLIENT Well, yes—isn't that what love is all about?

THERAPIST Let me ask you something—since your wife began working, have arrangements been made so that she doesn't have as many home responsibilities as she used to—do you take on more of the chores, do the children help?

CLIENT Well, no. I mean, I have a hard job and when I come home, I don't want to have to do housework. She understands that. Anyway, she never asks for help—I think she'd probably rather do it herself.

THERAPIST	Is it easy or difficult for her to take on all the household responsibilities and the children in the few hours she has every day after her job?
CLIENT	Well, she complains a lot, if that's what you mean. But I'm sure she doesn't expect me to help, if that's what you're leading up to. She just goes ahead and does what has to be done.
THERAPIST	Instead of talking with you . . .
CLIENT	Yes.
THERAPIST	Is it possible that one of *her* underlying beliefs is that if you really cared about her, you would notice how difficult two jobs are for her and offer to help?
CLIENT	I don't know.
THERAPIST	If you did help her, would that leave more time to talk?
CLIENT	I don't know—maybe I could ask her.

The type of therapy specifically developed to modify faulty beliefs is generally referred to as cognitive therapy or cognitive behaviour therapy. It focuses on teaching more effective cognitive skills. Ellis has developed his own very popular brand of therapy, Rational Emotive Therapy, which is designed to achieve this.

La vie en rose

Before we conclude that only socially ineffective people suffer from 'irrational' beliefs, we should consider some recent and fascinating research. It has been found that well-adjusted and socially skilled people often hold beliefs about themselves which are 'irrational', in the sense that they are not borne out by other people's opinions. These beliefs, however, turn out to be more *positive* than 'reality'. The self-image of depressed people, on the other hand, appears to be fairly close to the image others have of them. Perhaps what socially ineffective people badly need are the rose-coloured spectacles through which their more effective friends view the world!

Automatic but inappropriate

As we have already commented, much of our behaviour is so well learned or overlearned that it is automatic—we do not have to think about it. This is wonderful if we happen to be in situations where such automatic responses are appropriate. But if we produce these same responses in new or even slightly changed situations, where they are not called for, we prevent ourselves from generating more effective responses.

Social psychologist Fred Fiedler has done some very interesting research on the effects of experience and intelligence on effective behaviour in stressful situations. His results show that, in stressful situations, experience of similar sorts of situation is more helpful than intelligence. Why should this be? One of the effects of stress is that we tend to fall back on automatic or overlearned responses—we feel too pressured to think flexibly. People with experience of a wide range of social situations are likely to have a wide range of correct, or at least fairly effective, responses in their repertoire and are therefore better equipped automatically to produce appropriate responses under stress. Those with limited experience, however, are unlikely to be able to pull effective responses out of the hat at the right moment. In fact when highly intelligent people with little experience were under stress, Fiedler found that they tended to babble—most of what they said was irrelevant and disorganized. Their automatic chatter interfered with their proven ability, under less stressful circumstances, to solve problems.

Breaking automatic behaviour patterns is very difficult. By the time we realize what is happening, the behaviour is 'out', so to speak, and cannot be undone. To change these automatic patterns, one has to work very hard at spotting the events or situations which trigger off the automatic behaviour, then at stopping oneself launching into the automatic behaviour, and then at substituting more appropriate behaviour.

Choice model

According to this model our behaviour is the outcome of choice: we choose to sacrifice one type of effectiveness for another. For instance, we forego a specific goal in a situation (objective effectiveness) in order to avoid hurting another person (relationship and self-respect effectiveness). In any social interaction, a lot of juggling of goals and priorities goes on, with effectiveness in one area being traded for greater effectiveness in others. Refusing to choose is often a recipe for ineffectiveness, but trying to be effective across the board is an equally sure way of jeopardizing success—we all know people who are so over-extended that they do nothing very well.

Freedom to fail?

At times, we all give up trying to be effective—we are simply too tired, physically or emotionally. In such moods, our aims become unimportant. Nor is effectiveness particularly important if our goals are trivial, or if a relationship is casual. Really, the essence of the choice model is that we are perfectly free to choose a course of action which is ineffective. Only when we find ourselves making such choices a great deal of the time or when they become forced (remaining silent so as not to seem pushy, for example) does it become necessary to re-examine them. A person who finds herself always doing what others want and not what she wants may find she is losing touch with what her goals and individuality consist of, independent of other people.

When choice is limited

Finally, we should remember that no matter how

skilfully we behave, our environment often sets a limit on our choice of goals and relationships. Perhaps the most important limiting factor is our position in the power structure. Low-power people, with few resources at their disposal, must rely on their interactions with high-power people to attain their objectives. If a low-power person belongs to a group systematically discriminated against by those who control objectives and resources, he or she may be unable to attain them, no matter what social skills he or she has. A Roman Catholic woman, no matter how socially expert she is, is not going to achieve her objective if it requires ordainment to the priesthood. Many ethnic and political minorities achieve majority objectives (high salary, public recognition) through slow, private wars of attrition and often higher-than-average skills and strength of character. Discrimination comes in hundreds of guises, any of which can obstruct personal goals; age, race, sex, nationality, religion, socio-economic status, education, disablement—all of these things can limit the choices, the goals and the social skills a person develops. On occasion we all find ourselves in 'no-win' relationships.

4

Skills
for social success

Read the Apostles; they kissed everybody as a
form of greeting.

EMPRESS ALEXANDRA (1872–1918)

The first three chapters of this book have described
social interaction rather as if it were an obstacle course
negotiable only by the very lucky. In fact, the
'compleat social being' is probably a myth, an
unreasonable myth at that—nothing is as cloying as
complete success in any field. What we have been at
pains to demonstrate is that effective behaviour
involves a multiplicity of skills and that piecemeal
examination of behaviour can help us to reduce or
even avoid the pitfalls. In this and the following three
chapters, we look closer at these skills.

Before ever we say a word or raise a finger, that is,
behave overtly, we have already performed a number
of skilled behaviours, those which psychologists
categorize as cognitive or physiological. Usually we
are completely, and mercifully, unaware of all this
inner activity—if we were to give as much thought to
the social routine of greeting friends as to approaching
our bank manager for a loan, smooth social interaction
would be impossible. But, as we pointed out in

Chapter 2, smoothly executed behaviours involve not fewer skills, but skills which have been perfected to the point of becoming second nature.

Skills related to thinking

Because of their relative importance, we begin with cognitive skills, describing each of them in turn. The skills which come into the cognitive category can be summarized as SJS—Sensitivity, Judgement and Self-regulation.

Sensitivity

What do we mean when we describe someone as socially sensitive? Usually that they are able to pick up fairly subtle cues from people and settings which tell them exactly what is going on. 'The boss is in a bad mood today', 'Those two obviously like each other' or 'It's time for me to leave' are samples of the running commentary that goes on inside our head as we pick up these little signals. But how accurate are our antennae? Very rarely does our host say 'I would like you to leave now', and yet, using non-verbal signals— perhaps glancing at his watch, or not offering more coffee—he has conveyed to us that he would like us to go. He is probably unaware that he is giving these signals, and we for our part are probably only half aware of them—much non-verbal communication works at a level little below conscious awareness.

It is precisely because this sort of communication lacks the explicitness of words that misinterpretations occur. Bruce Orvis, for example, has shown that couples often jump to wrong conclusions about their partner's behaviour (silences, for example) and behave inappropriately as a result. To quote one of Orvis's specific findings, couples quite often interpret each other's behaviour in a way which contradicts what is actually said, and particularly so when behaviour is 'negative'. One partner returns home, slumps into a chair, and says: 'It's been a lousy day. I feel worn out.' Nine times out of ten that is the truth—no 'game' is being played. But the partner immediately thinks: 'He/she doesn't care about me'; nine times out of ten that is not true, and the behaviour that follows is inappropriate. People with low self-esteem ('I've only been invited to make up the numbers') also behave inappropriately.

As we noted in Chapter 2, making correct assumptions about the behaviour of another person is not easy—their thoughts and feelings are not transparent,

A GUIDE FOR SENSITIVE PEOPLE.

1. A BOSS IN A BAD MOOD.

nor do they necessarily match overt behaviour. Nor do obvious signals always mean the same thing in the same individual; Michael Argyle and his colleagues at Oxford University have shown, for example, that avoiding looking someone in the eye may mean that you are (a) anxious, (b) bored, (c) embarrassed, (d) angry, or (e) very attracted to them.

What the socially sensitive person does is observe people's behaviour very closely, picking up as wide a variety of cues as possible so as not to jump to premature conclusions.

If you constantly encounter insensitivity in others, or find your intentions are constantly misinterpreted, think carefully about your visible behaviour and whether it matches what you are thinking and feeling. Could the signals you are giving—your overt behaviour—be considered misleading? Remember Woody Allen's experience in the film *Play it again, Sam*? He dated a lady whose overt behaviour was very seductive, took her home, and after a session on his couch suggested that they go to bed; her response was to slap his face and demand 'What kind of woman do you think I am?' Her signals were obviously totally misleading. A rather extreme example, certainly, but therapists often find that people who complain about not being understood are in fact giving out wrong or deceptive signals.

Sensitivity, like judgement and self-regulation, is not a general trait—it is possible to be highly sensitive in one situation and not in another. Frieda W., a lawyer, is often asked to handle delicate negotiations between international corporations buying and selling oil. She shows uncanny skill in sensing just how far a negotiator is willing to go to make a deal, or when he or she is beginning to feel pressured. She also has a teenage son, but with him she constantly battles over curfews, tidiness and other house rules. Her sensitivity does not seem to stretch to realizing that her son wants to be more independent.

Social judgement

If we sum up a situation wrongly, our overt behaviour is unlikely to be effective. But if we are right, it does not necessarily follow that we will do the right thing. A friend may be upset, but knowing it and doing something about it are two different things. Social judgement is, in essence, thinking out a plan of action and imagining what effect it will have, so a number of different skills are involved: thinking of several different courses of action which might be appropriate (leave the friend alone, offer a shoulder to cry on, try to cheer them up); weighing up the possible outcomes of these different alternatives (the friend may be grateful for privacy or sympathy, or feel that you don't care); and knowing how these alternatives and their outcomes are going to affect you. (Do you *want* to

2. A MAN DISPLAYING NEGATIVE
BEHAVIOUR.

encourage your friends to bring problems to you? Are you going to feel guilty if you leave them feeling miserable?)

Tests have shown that the social judgement skills of children and adolescents are related to a number of other measures of adjustment at school, notably academic performance, attendance and participation in extra-curricular activities. Indeed, the comprehensive programme which has been constructed for teaching these skills to schoolchildren could be applied, with great benefit, to adults as well. Part of this programme involves presenting a 'situation' to the child—for a five-year-old this might be 'Johnnie has run off with your ball', or for a fifteen-year-old 'You and your parents always disagree about when you should come home at night'—and asking the child to think up a number of ways of reacting (no matter how bizarre) and to consider what the outcomes might be. Adult self-help groups and a number of therapy groups also use this strategy. When we talk of learning from other people, we really mean that they spark off new ideas about how we might behave and give us a foretaste of the possible results.

Another vital element in the judgement process is knowing whether or not you can actually carry out the behaviours you have thought up. Be realistic. It is no good deciding to tell jokes to impress someone and then realizing, too late, that you have forgotten the punchlines. Part of good judgement is the thinking through of actions in advance, the step-by-step approach: in order to apply for a new job, you first have to write or telephone, then prepare a curriculum vitae, then go for one or more interviews—the goal is getting a job, but several stages of action are involved. We are not suggesting that every interaction requires a well thought out, step-by-step approach, but situations we find difficult, and behaviours we wish to change, often do.

Self-regulation
We have talked about sensitivity and judgement as

skills which precede overt behaviour, but they continue to be used—in the same way that a tightrope walker uses a balancing pole—at every stage of an interaction. They are the tools we use to regulate our behaviour moment by moment. Self-regulation is therefore the act of combining both external information (she's interested, she's bored, she'd like to change the subject) and internal information (I'll keep talking, I'll yawn and then he'll leave, I can't put this one off). It is most disconcerting to be faced with someone who does not integrate these two sources of information— we think we have made it clear that the interaction is over or that we don't want to talk about something, and they carry on regardless. Salesmen, of course, are successful precisely because they are trained *not* to

3. HOW TO RECOGNISE a BORING PARTY..

regulate their behaviour in response to off-putting cues.

A second, more global, aspect of self-regulation—often called self-control—is our ability to put off desired, immediate outcomes in favour of longer-term objectives. We stop ourselves from quarrelling with a friend over some irrelevant issue, we build up goodwill with a client by carrying promises out promptly, we stay at a boring party rather than hurt the hostess's feelings. Since many of our interactions span long periods, and many of our goals are long-range, the importance of self-control skills should not be underestimated.

George P. is a man who is always searching for the ultimate, intimate relationship. He doesn't understand what happens when someone he has been dating a few times decides to stop seeing him. George wants a stable, exclusive, long-term relationship, which he makes clear to the women he goes out with on the first date. He makes the kind of disclosures on a first date that most people reserve for relationships that are well established and have a history of bonding. Some of the women George goes out with are also interested in the kind of stable relationship he seeks, but they shy away from the demands of immediate intimacy he places on them from the beginning. George does not regulate his desire for intimacy, gradually increasing the closeness over time; he comes across to potential mates as someone so needy as to be indiscriminate in his choice of partners and in his desire for closeness. George would do well to delay intimacy demands in the service of more satisfactory long-term gains.

Cognitive skills are therefore a prelude and accompaniment to every social interaction and are bound up with each other in a very complex way. But given the equal complexity of the social environment, and the subtlety of some of the cues we respond to, a simple set of skills would hardly be equal to the task!

Emotional skills

Some of our most intense emotional experiences—love, grief, fear of rejection, pity, guilt—arise through our relationships with others and, inescapably, they are bound up with the thought processes we have just been discussing.

Emotions, and the physiological responses which accompany them, are linked with social effectiveness in several ways. Ideally, our emotional equipment should include the ability to experience a wide range of emotions, the ability to control our emotions, and the ability to label other people's emotions correctly.

Emotional range

Common sense tells us that if someone has never experienced grief or fear of rejection, they will be ill-equipped to sympathize with someone who is grief-stricken or fearful, or even to predict the kind of situation or behaviour likely to cause these emotional states. If we rarely experience joy, we may lack the ability to respond enthusiastically to others—as we saw in Chapter 3, this would come under the heading of 'failure to reinforce' others for mixing with us. To prove the truth of this, one has only to be at the receiving end of someone else's lack of emotion. In fact, our range of emotions is widest when we are in environments which respond to us. Depressed people are not responsive and so have a mood-lowering effect on those around them. Not only that, but their unresponsiveness dissuades others from responding to them, which makes them even less responsive, and the vicious circle is established.

Emotional control

Intense emotion, which easily disorganizes our thinking and interferes with the application of proven skills, can be controlled by positive thought strategies—concentrating hard on the other person so that you forget your own feelings, imagining pleasant (but realistic) outcomes to the situation, rehearsing likely topics of conversation beforehand—but these demand a great deal of practice. On the whole it is fair to say that most people find it easier to cope with inhibiting feelings by practising relaxation, yoga, or one of the modern methods of meditation.

At the other end of the spectrum are individuals who are emotionally apathetic to the point of hardly responding to other people at all. Deeply preoccupied with themselves, they miss many social cues and give very little in the way of reinforcement or feedback to others. The idea that depression and apathy can be positively managed is fairly new, but researchers Peter Lewinshon and Lyn Rehm have both devised ways of doing this. These include relaxation training and scheduling 'positive' activities—depressed people, though they are often not aware of it, spend a lot of time doing things they don't enjoy, things which have a negative, mood-convincing effect.

Emotional labelling

A wide variety of emotions masquerade under very similar physiological states. Anxiety, anger, sexual arousal or pleasurable anticipation are all accompanied by a faster heart-beat, but only we know for sure what we are feeling. Another person has only our visible animation or agitation to go by, and their knowledge of our personality and the events concerned. If they interpret our flushed face as anger instead of embarrassment, they will behave inappropriately towards us. Being good at inferring emotions means paying a lot of attention to the situation and to other aspects of people's behaviour before drawing any conclusions.

However, inferences about another person's feelings are seldom one hundred per cent reliable. The easiest, and most obvious, way of finding out what someone is feeling is to ask them. This is exactly what 'good with people' people do. Imagining oneself in the other person's shoes is another approach, not always reliable perhaps, but a good exercise in sensitivity. What does it feel to be pressured by a wife and burst water pipes at home, a car that won't start, and new responsibilities and next to impossible deadlines at work?

What others see

The third of our behaviour categories, by far the most important in social situations, is overt behaviour, behaviour that can be seen or heard by another person. Exquisite sensitivity to social nuances and to other people's feelings, impeccable *savoir faire* or knowing all the rules, and the actions expected of us—these are all useless unless we put them into practice.

There is no 'correct' behaviour for every situation . . . which is not what books on etiquette would have us believe. There is only behaviour which is more or less effective in terms of the goals we consciously or unconsciously formulate for ourselves. And goals change with time and place and mood. Since these goals cannot be achieved by pure thought or pure knowledge or pure emotion, we can now move on to consider the overt behaviour skills which help us to pursue the three types of goals we have already talked about: achieving material objectives, building satisfying relationships, and keeping our self-respect. Take a look at the following list of more and less effective behavioural moves or strategies and see if you can recognize them at work in your own life:

More effective	Less effective
Develop more awareness of the small cues which indicate what is 'going on' in social situations.	Notice only what people say, and ignore non-verbal signals.

More effective	Less effective
Realize that the same behaviour can mean a variety of things.	Jump to instant conclusions about the meaning of people's behaviour.
Remember that people's thoughts, feelings and behaviour don't always match.	Assume that you can tell exactly what people are feeling and thinking.
Don't give cues which are likely to be misinterpreted.	Assume that others can read your mind and will always understand what you are doing.
Recognize that there are different ways of dealing with any situation.	Stick rigidly to the same methods of dealing with people and situations.
Think through the possible outcomes of your behaviour.	Act first and think later.
Know your limitations.	Try new behaviours which seem to work for others without knowing whether *you* can carry them off.
Pay careful attention to verbal and non-verbal feedback from others and adjust your behaviour accordingly	Assume that what you have to say or do is more important than what others are trying to 'tell' you.
Postpone desired immediate outcomes in favour of important long-term objectives.	Act impulsively according to the mood of the moment.
Mix with people who respond positively to you and to life generally.	Mix with cynics and pessimists.

More effective	Less effective
Remember that people will not respond positively to you unless you respond positively to them.	Assume that other people's reactions to you have nothing to do with yours to them.
Make some attempt to control strong emotions.	Feel helpless in the face of your emotions.
Concentrate on what other people are saying and doing as a way of reducing your own anxiety or nervousness.	Concentrate on your own actions and feelings to the exclusion of other people's.
Think through situations in advance and anticipate problems and your handling of them.	Tackle situations without forethought and allow yourself to be swept along by them.
Practise some method of relaxation even if it is only deep breathing in moments of stress.	Make no conscious effort to control anxiety, anger, frustration.
If you are uncertain of other people's thoughts and feelings, ask them what they are thinking or feeling, or else try to imagine yourself in their situation.	Assume that if people want you to know what they are thinking or feeling, they will tell you.

A cognitive skills task

Now let's look at a particular situation. Imagine that you are at a party, and want to join a group of people who are already talking together. Two factors should influence your decision as to whether in fact you do

join the group and, in particular, *how* you do so. First
there is the matter of *sensitivity*: do you think that the
group will accept a new member? Secondly, there is a
question of *judgement*: which, of all the alternative
ways of joining the group, is likely to be the most
effective?

Sensitivity

Question: what is going on within the group you want to
join? Or more specifically, is the group 'open' (in which case
a new member would be welcome) or is it 'closed'
(unreceptive to new members)?

Open	Closed
Everyone standing somewhat apart	Everyone standing close together
Members occasionally glance around the room	Members attending exclusively to each other
Gaps in the conversation	Very animated conversation with few gaps
Group talking about a topic of general interest	Members seem to be 'pairing off'

Judgement

Question: do you join the group or not? If the group is open
your decision is Yes, if closed No. More specifically, what
are the alternative ways of joining the group and what are
their likely outcomes?

Ways of joining the group	Outcomes
Move gradually closer to the group.	It may not be clear, from the slowness of your approach, that you want to join them; it might even look as if you were creeping up and trying to eavesdrop!

Ways of joining the group	Outcomes
Offer to refill their glasses / hand round food.	That could be overdoing things a bit. What would you do if they refused more food / drink? Even if they didn't, would you have made it clear enough that you wanted to join the group?
Stand beside them and chip in on their conversation.	That might seem rude—they haven't 'invited' you to join them; and anyway, what exactly are you going to say when you chip in? Have you got the nerve?
Go up and introduce yourself.	Isn't that over-formal? Having introduced yourself, then what do you say? Will they introduce themselves to you? Wouldn't you interrupt the flow of conversation? In any case, do you have the self-confidence to introduce yourself?
Wait for a lull in the conversation, stand beside a friendly-looking member of the group, and say something like 'Mind if I join you?'	This makes your intention clear and doesn't seem rude or interrupt the conversation; the members of the group can then choose whether to introduce themselves or not.

Self-regulation

Question: which of all the options above will you implement?

5

Getting the things you want

The secret of success is constancy of purpose.

BENJAMIN DISRAELI (1804–1881)

Let us look at the negative side of the coin first: no one ever got what they wanted, or got other people to do what they wanted, by being unclear about their objectives, afraid to stand up for them, or unduly swayed by the needs and wishes of others. Objective effectiveness involves all the opposite behaviours: having a clear picture of what you want, being assertive, and resisting the influence of others.

Assertiveness is often confused with aggression or selfishness, but it is neither. To be assertive is to stand up for oneself, while taking other people's interests and feelings into account, and not to be thrown off balance by other people's aggressive or selfish behaviour. George Bernard Shaw's remark that the 'effectiveness of assertion is the alpha and omega of style' comes very close to the truth: assertion only works when it is implemented with sensitivity and style. Women often have a harder time being assertive than men. Paula Caplan of Toronto University has reviewed a number of studies which suggest that many women are more eager to please others than to please themselves, which means a heavy sacrifice of important objectives.

As for resisting influence, it is sometimes difficult to tell when resisting it turns into exercising it. When you return your defective week-old shoes, you are trying to influence the manager to refund you the money, but he or she is trying to persuade you to have the shoes repaired.

Whether or not we realize it, we are continuously influencing and being influenced in our day-to-day encounters. As we have seen, our behaviour is very much a product of our environment: as we form part of other people's environment, so we cannot help but influence their behaviour. Becoming more aware of this mutual influence is an essential part of increasing both objective and relationship effectiveness.

There are no prescribed behaviours for exercising or resisting influence—both culture and situation determine those for any particular occasion. Accordingly, the purpose of this chapter is to give the reader some

systematic way of analysing interactions and to suggest how objective effectiveness might be increased no matter what the situation or cultural context.

Influencing others

Three important points should be borne in mind in any attempt to exert influence.

1 What is it that you want to achieve?

If you ask a friend for a favour, return flawed merchandise, or ask for a raise, you probably think you know exactly what you want to achieve. But consider this exchange:

A I bought this kettle yesterday and it doesn't work. I'd like a refund.
B The manager isn't here just now.
A I'm not asking for the manager. I want you to take this kettle back.
B But I've got a lot of customers to serve.
A It's disgraceful how customers are treated these days . . .

Although A would have said that his or her goal was clear—to obtain a refund—it was quickly lost sight of and exchanged for a different one—expressing anger at customer relations. If A had pursued the original goal, the interaction might have gone like this:

A I bought this kettle yesterday and it doesn't work. I'd like a refund.
B The manager isn't here just now.
A Is it only the manager who deals with refunds?
B Yes. I've got a lot of customers to serve.
A When will the manager be available to arrange the refund?

Losing sight of original goals is a very common reason for failing to achieve them. Of course, the person you are trying to influence often tries to make you lose sight of your goal—the manager, for example, may persuade A to have the kettle repaired. So it is important to know how far you are willing to compromise—to accept a new kettle as a replacement, but not to have the old one repaired.

Goals also have to be stated clearly. Indirect statements rely too much on the sensitivity of the other person to work reliably. Often we fail to get what we want because other people do not *know* what we want, not because they do not want to give it. Suppose you are in a stuffy room and the only window is closed. You could try the direct approach and say: 'I'm hot, would you mind if I opened the window?' or the indirect approach: 'Are you hot? Do you want me to open a window?' In either case, the other person may say the opposite of what you want, but if your approach was direct, you will at least know that your message was understood. If you disguise your thoughts and feelings you are setting the other person a very difficult task, and should not be surprised if you are misunderstood. This is not to say that indirect techniques are never useful or successful, just that there are times when it is better to hold your cards close to your chest. But it is important to know which technique, direct or indirect, you are using.

2 What kind of relationship do you want?

Any attempt to influence others will affect your relationship with them. It is here that objective and relationship effectiveness meet and where social judgement skills become very important. If you can think of a number of alternative behaviours likely to achieve your goal and can predict what effect they will have on you and on the other person, you will have gone a long way towards achieving objective and relationship effectiveness.

In any interaction, even if you will never see the person again, you are more likely to achieve your goal if your relationship with them is good. You cannot simply decide that you will demand things from people you don't know and ask nicely for them from people you do.

It has been shown that assertive behaviour is seldom judged to be effective unless it is accompanied by a smile. Similarly, one of the authors found that most Americans rate empathic requests, requests which show concern for the other person's feelings (I know you're very busy, but I'd be grateful if you could . . .') as more effective than blunt demands. But in America, at least, an effusively apologetic request (I'm terribly sorry to bother you, I know you must be very busy, but . . .') is considered less effective.

To maintain a good relationship, it is often necessary to compromise one's original goal and to trade reinforcers, a process psychologists call 'reciprocity'. Someone who gets what they want and maintains satisfying relationships usually keeps a cognitive 'balance sheet', a mental account of services given and received, and is careful not to get too overdrawn ('If you have the children today, I'll do the shopping for both of us' or 'You had the children last week, so I'll have them today'). One extensive study of how the balance sheet principle operates in marriage has concluded that its breakdown is one of the major causes of marital discord. In an unhappy marriage the 'balance' seems to go wrong in two ways: either one partner feels that they are doing all the 'giving' and getting very little in return, or the balance sheet principle only operates in a negative way, with only 'slights', never 'boosts', being reciprocated. In a happy marriage the tendency is for far more positive than negative trading. Developing positive rather than negative reciprocity between partners is one approach to marital therapy.

3 Who has the power?

Crudely speaking, the more powerful person in a relationship controls important resources and rewards which they can distribute or withhold as they please. We often think of powerful people as those who control material things. But if you love or care about someone, they have power over you because they control important emotional reinforcers. Similarly, if someone cares about you, you have power over them. Power can also be temporary or bestowed by the situation: you have more power over a chain smoker in a non-smoking area than in an area where smoking is allowed.

So the power relationships between people inevitably help or hinder their attempts to get what they want. Only people in positions of power can punish— by threats, criticism, prosecution, violence, withholding important reinforcers such as praise, status and money. And in a relationship where the balance of power is unequal, punishment is a very successful method of achieving objectives, but it just as successfully destroys relationships. Nevertheless, low-power people have their weapons—children and adults sulk, a bored and resentful wife pleads headaches to avoid sex. Indeed Ihsan Al-Issa of Calgary University has suggested that many 'neurotic' behaviours are actually ways in which low-power people exercise influence.

Of course power is not always exercised negatively, nor are powerful people always disliked. If you exercise power, you can supply great reinforcements to others, which in turn reinforces you. Reciprocity is the key to all good relationships. Even powerful people long to be loved.

Resisting influence

There are several reasons why resisting influence can be difficult. First of all, how do you spot attempts to influence you? Often one is the target of considerable forethought—the influencer has the luxury of advance planning, but you do not. You have to think quickly. What is it you are being asked to do? As we have seen, requests are often made vaguely or indirectly ('I'm looking for someone to help out . . . ', or 'I hear you're very good at . . . ') so how do you know whether you want to say No? So the first ploy must be to clarify the nature of the request. You must also know how much you are prepared to compromise ('No, I can't help this week, but I can next week' or 'I never lend my gramophone records, but you're welcome to play them here').

Having decided on your ultimate point of resistance, there is still the problem of remaining firm and not getting side-tracked. There is one way of doing this which is so straightforward, and so effective, that it is often overlooked. Manuel Smith, a Los Angeles clinical psychologist, calls it the 'broken record technique': you politely repeat your initial refusal in the face of side-tracking, threats or compliments, until the other person accepts it.

A Could you stay tonight and finish this work?
B I'm sorry, but I won't be able to stay.
A But it's important and you're the only one who can do it.
B I'm sorry about that, but I can't work late.
A But you're usually so reliable.
B Yes. But tonight I just can't stay.

Compare this with an exchange where the technique is not used:

A Can you stay tonight and finish this work?
B I'm sorry, but I can't.
A But it's important and you're the only one who can do it.
B I'd like to . . . but I have guests coming.
A Couldn't you ring them and say you'll be a bit late?
B Well, I don't like to do that.
A I'm sure they won't mind if you say how important it is. You can have the morning off instead.
B Well . . .
A Great. I'm glad you can stay.

Of course, the first exchange could be softened by adding 'I have guests coming' or 'I'll do it first thing tomorrow' but these embellishments must not obscure your repeated refusal, otherwise you will lose sight of your goal, to say No, and end up saying Yes.

Not feeling guilty about saying No

Saying No does not necessarily earn dislike, but how and why you say No is important. So often a person's rationale for not refusing favours is that people will stop liking them. But if you say No with a smile, expressing some understanding of the other person's problem (but implying that you are not the person to solve it) and have good reason for refusing, there is very little chance of the relationship being damaged. On the other hand, if you refuse curtly, or make the other

HOW TO SAY NO...

person feel guilty for having asked ('I helped last year . . . isn't it someone else's turn?' or 'I don't let people borrow my books . . . they never return them'), they will almost certainly like you less, not for having refused but for having made them feel bad.

What if your reason for refusing is selfish, or simply cannot be expressed ('No one ever returns my books and I don't think you will either')? In such cases it is still appropriate to refuse firmly but politely (use the broken record technique). It is how you say No which minimizes risk to the relationship (I'm sorry, but it's a personal rule of mine never to lend books').

Why then is there a general reluctance to take No for an answer? One reason is that refusals are often indirect ('I'd like to help', 'I don't know . . . ', 'I'll have to think about it'), so indirect that the other person may not realize that their request is being refused. Even if the message is a polite and unequivocal No, most of us know from experience that persistence sometimes pays—if we nag long enough we often get what we want.

If a child learns that a two-hour temper tantrum sometimes gets what she or he wants, an initial refusal will not be a deterrent. So instead of blaming other people for not taking No as your final answer, you should consider how often you give way after a first No. If your No's are bendable, you are actually encouraging others to persist in the face of refusal. The mechanism at work here is one which psychologists call 'intermittent reinforcement'—certain behaviours persist far longer if they are only rewarded now and then, not all the time. Every time you say No, and then say Yes, however grudgingly, you make it more difficult for yourself to resist influence. You are also making it more difficult for less strong-minded individuals to hold out in the face of persistent influence.

What we have seen in this chapter is that it is possible to achieve important objectives, or resist attempts to gain them from you, while still maintaining good relationships. There is, of course, much more to making and keeping relationships than this. The next chapter explores ways of doing this, when the objective is the relationship itself.

More effective	Less effective
Make a distinction between assertiveness and aggressiveness or selfishness.	Think that your wants and needs always come second to everyone else's.
Recognize that exerting and resisting influence demands a clear idea of what you want to achieve.	Continually modify your goals in response to other people's demands.
State clearly what you want.	Beat about the bush, make indirect requests.
Always make requests politely.	Make demands, not requests.
Don't apologize for making requests.	Precede every request with an apology.
Not only make requests but be prepared to do favours in return.	Don't return favours.
Avoid criticism, threats and sulking as methods of exerting or resisting influence.	Rely on negative techniques—criticism, threats, getting angry—to influence others.
Recognize quickly when others are trying to influence you and clarify what is being asked of you.	Comply with vague general requests and then feel resentful and 'used' afterwards.
Know exactly how much you are willing to give/do.	Have no clear idea about how far you are prepared to fall in with others' suggestions or requests.

More effective	Less effective
Don't allow yourself to be side-tracked into granting requests you really want to refuse.	Allow your refusals to become weaker and weaker.
Recognize that saying No and meaning No will reduce pressure from others in the future.	Blame other people for not taking No for an answer.
Accept that everyone has the right to say No; saying No is not a crime.	Feel guilty about saying No.
Refuse requests as politely as possible.	Make others feel bad about making requests.

6

Making and keeping relationships

We're left alone with each other. We have to
creep close to each other and give those gentle
little nudges with our paws and our muzzles
before we can slip into sleep and rest for the
next day's playtime . . . and the next day's
mysteries.

TENNESSEE WILLIAMS (b. 1914)

Material goals (borrowing a car, returning faulty
goods) are usually quite easy to define in advance, and
success or failure is usually quite easy to define
afterwards. If, however, our goal in an interaction or
in a series of interactions is to create or maintain a
positive relationship with another person, it is much
more difficult to say exactly what 'positive' is or when
we can regard that goal as having been achieved.

There is a general tendency not to think of relationships in terms of overt behaviour; instead, we
talk about feelings and attitudes ('I trust her', 'He cares
about me', 'I'm being taken for granted'). However,
examined closely, these statements are not direct data,
but inferences from overt behaviour. We know that
someone cares about us because of certain things they
say and do, although we might have to think hard
before we can pinpoint the behaviour which leads us

to this conclusion. If we are to form new relationships, however, or strengthen existing ones, we *must* attend to overt behaviour. It is what people say and do to each other which creates bonds between them.

Social and clinical psychologists have devoted a lot of energy to studying just what it is that draws people together and drives them apart. Unfortunately, much of this research has been carried out using limited samples of people: social psychologists tend to study volununteer college students, while clinical psycholo-

The reason we get on so well is that we both LOVE me...

gists concentrate on people who already have relationship problems. The results, however, are surprisingly consistent. Although there is a lot we do not know, the knowledge we have can be applied to good effect in many different settings.

Getting people to like you

How are people supposed to like you, or you them, if you do not see them or speak to them? This simple fact, the fact of physical proximity, is often overlooked.

Proximity and opportunity

Social psychologists Leon Festinger, Stanley Schachter and Kurt Back showed conclusively that proximity favours friendship by studying the development of relationships in a new housing project for married students. The houses were arranged in U-shaped courts with the two end houses of each U facing the street and the rest overlooking a grassy area. None of the student couples who moved in when term started had met before, so the setting was tailor-made for studying the development of friendships. Festinger and Schachter found that two factors were very important: the distances between houses, and the direction in which they faced. Couples who were friendly tended to live quite close together, but the poor occupants of the houses facing the street had less than half the number of friends that everyone else had. The couples with most friends were those whose houses were on the busiest passing routes. It was not their personal attributes or friendly disposition which brought them friends, but their geographical position and the frequency with which people passed their doors.

There is now a large body of research in both Britain and America which adds weight to these findings. It does not seem to matter *why* people are brought together—in one study it was because their names began with the same letter of the alphabet. The results are always the same: we make friends with people we see most often.

A first step in forming new relationships, therefore, is to ask yourself: what opportunities do I have to make casual but regular contact with people? Do you share an office? Does your desk face the wall or the centre of the room? Do you wait until the crowd has gone before you use the elevator or the coffee machine? Do you live in a house or an apartment? Given a choice of job or housing, you can opt for more

Did you know that social psychologists say that PROXIMITY favours friendship?

or fewer opportunities to make contact with others. Mundane as it sounds, a lot of people find many of their friends among neighbours and work colleagues.

Similarity

What determines whether we like the people we come into contact with? One very energetic researcher into why we like some people more than others, has given one answer: almost always we like those who share our attitudes. The saying that 'opposites attract' may be true occasionally, but for most of us, most of the time, it isn't. Insignificant attitudes—the brand of toothpaste you like—can usually be discounted. Really important attitudes, attitudes to wider issues such as politics, life-style, morals and so on, are the ones which matter. One reason why many attempts to bring people together are only partly successful is that the characteristics on which groups are based (age, single parenthood) are unrelated to these attitudes. Groups are often less similar than they might appear.

The fact that similarity is a powerful link between people does not mean you will be more attractive to people if you agree with them all the time. What it does mean is that you should seek opportunities to mix with people whose attitudes are similar and, when you discover them, be sure to let them know it. Attitude similarity probably induces liking because it reinforces our view of the world. Having one's views endorsed is very reinforcing.

In various studies of married couples the partners of happy marriages have been found to be more similar than partners who separate or divorce. It may be, of course, that couples grow more similar with time. What is particularly interesting, however, is that if asked about each other's attitudes, happily married people tend to assume they are more similar than they actually are, while dissatisfied couples appear more aware of their differences.

However, similarity and liking do not always go together. It has been found that if someone who is similar to us also has something unattractive about

89

them (such as having been in prison or in a mental hospital), we tend to like them less than someone who is dissimilar, but has nothing unattractive about them. In this case, the similarity is threatening: it does not really validate our view of the world, and suggests that we too are vulnerable.

Conversation skills

The art of conversation has been largely neglected by psychologists. On the other hand non-verbal communication—eye gaze, facial expression, posture—has been very extensively investigated. Certainly, non-verbal communication is very important, but it is difficult to keep smiling if you don't know what to say. Even skilled eye gaze does not enliven a boring monologue.

Fortunately, psychologists are now showing more interest in conversation skills. Minkin, for example, found that three behaviours were typical of people who were rated 'good conversationalists'. These were: asking plenty of questions, giving 'positive feedback' (indicating that you have heard, understood and appreciated what the other person says), and speaking for more than half the conversation time. This last is a very sensitive measure: good conversationalists do tend to talk more, but talking more means taking up a *bit* more than 50 per cent of total speaking time, not all of it!

Questions, answers and compliments

J.A. Kelly and his associates found that three skills in particular helped people who were having problems in making relationships: these were asking questions (as Minkin had found), giving personal information, and paying compliments. A third study, by Tom Kupke of Tulsa University, also underlined the importance of asking questions: men who asked women questions about themselves were considered more attractive than men who talked about themselves or responded with short, non-specific statements such as 'Oh, really'.

There is, of course, a thin line between asking questions skilfully and turning a conversation into an interrogation session. If both speakers are skilled, the questions tend to be reciprocated:

A Do you know many people here?
B No. I'm a friend of Jane's. Do you know her too?
A No, but I'm friendly with her husband—we work together. How did you get to know Jane?
B We were neighbours before they moved here. Are you a teacher like John?

Compare this with an exchange where only one person asks the questions:

A Do you know many people here?
B No, I don't.
A Are you a friend of Jane's?
B I know her, but not very well.
A How do you know her?
B We work together.

One reason why the first exchange seems altogether smoother and easier (and results in greater liking) is that A and B are not only asking each other questions, but also volunteering more information than is actually asked for, which quite naturally leads to more questions. There has been a great deal of research into how talking about ourselves can lead others to like or dislike us. Appropriate self-disclosure, not too much and not too little, requires social sensitivity and social judgement. As relationships progress, there is a tendency to disclose more and more about ourselves, but too little or too much at the wrong time can decrease liking. We seem to like each other best when we disclose roughly the same amount and kind of information. If you feel that you never manage to get close to people, you may be missing their 'disclosing' cues (a failure of sensitivity) and not revealing enough about yourself. On the other hand, if people seem to 'back off' after a short time, perhaps you are giving too much personal information too soon. It is a moot point whether therapy groups which encourage people to be very open about themselves actually teach a behaviour which is an asset; very often we do not want to hear a person's life history at first meeting.

Answering questions in a 'closed' fashion and revealing too much too soon are both breaches of the many 'rules' of good and enjoyable conversation. People who find it difficult to talk to others or who report that others don't seem to enjoy talking to them, are usually, without realizing it, breaking some of these rules. Do you, for example, begin most of your sentences with 'I'? If so, your listeners will find you much less likable than if you comment on what they say before steering the conversation back to yourself. Do you interrupt? This need not always mean breaking into someone's sentences—if you start talking just fractionally before or instantly after someone has finished, you risk giving the impression that you are not really listening to them, only waiting for them to be quiet so that you can have your say!

Because the differences between good and poor conversationalists can be very subtle, a helpful exercise is to imagine several people you would classify as one or the other and try to list all the things about their conversation which makes them enjoyable, or unpleasant, to talk to.

However, what if the problem is not that you don't know the rules of good conversation, but that you simply do not know what to talk about? For some people this means not being sure which topics are appropriate for which situations. Unfortunately there are no hard-and-fast rules here—what is needed are sensitivity and judgement skills (observing which topics are being discussed and how people react to them). For others the 'what to talk about' problem has more to do with lack of activity: the person who has few hobbies, does not keep abreast of current affairs, rarely ventures out to the theatre or the cinema or abroad will have little to contribute to conversation. Nor does conversation have to be deeply meaningful to be enjoyable. The value of 'small talk' should not be underestimated. Students in one experiment who were asked to get to know each other without using small talk found the task impossible. They simply didn't know where to begin.

Expressing liking

One very important piece of information we can give about ourselves is how much we like another person.

I've been your mistress for five years, read four books on LIKING PEOPLE, attended three analysts, and two groups – BUT I STILL CAN'T STAND YOU!

We can do this in several ways: tell them directly, praise or compliment them, seek their company, and listen to them. The finding that we like people who express liking for us is as consistent as the finding that we like people who share our attitudes. This 'reciprocity of liking' rule, however, has several refinements.

First, we tend to react most positively to people who praise us for attributes we would like to have but are not quite sure we possess, *not* for attributes we wished we had but know very well we haven't. But it can take considerable sensitivity to work out what these wished-for qualities are in a person. On the other hand, liking is not necessarily increased by remarking on totally obvious characteristics, on the intelligence of someone with a double first and a PhD, for example, or on the driving skills of someone who has just failed their test for the third time.

Secondly, although we are inclined to accept praise and liking at face value, we sometimes get suspicious. Are they like that with everyone? Most of us like to think we are special, so to be liked by someone who likes everyone is no great honour. Are they sincere? Do they have an ulterior motive?

Expressing liking for someone you are dependent on is called 'ingratiation', and the psychologist who has devoted most study to the process has been Edward Jones of Princeton University. If the recipient of the ingratiation knows that the other person wants something from them, the person doing the ingratiating is generally disliked. In situations where the extent of one person's dependence on the other is unclear, the results of ingratiation are less predictable.

Expressing liking, therefore, is not always a straightforward process. The rules seem to be that we should comment on less obvious attributes, not be too lavish or too frequent in our praise, never use compliments to obtain favours, express liking privately, or at least selectively, and remember Oscar Wilde's dictum that 'a little sincerity is a dangerous thing and a great deal of it is absolutely fatal'.

Place and time

Because association is such a powerful factor in learning, it follows that being with people when they experience positive emotions (or relief from negative emotions such as fear or loneliness) links us in their mind with good, strong feelings. William Griffit and his associates, for example, found that people reacted far less positively to strangers when they were in a hot, humid room than when they were in a cool, comfortable one. The lesson implicit here is that one should accompany the people one likes or would like to like, to events they enjoy, on the principle that the enjoyment of the occasion will attach itself to you. We tend to do this naturally at the beginning of relationships, but get lazier as they progress.

An interesting variation on this idea is that the attraction between people is often stronger if they meet in circumstances where they are experiencing some emotional arousal. In one experiment, men who met a woman in the middle of a swaying rope bridge rated her as more attractive than men who met her on dry land. The men on the bridge, it seems, mislabelled their fear (raised heart-beat, dizziness) as attraction. This labelling process is often misleading: as the song puts it 'This can't be love . . . because I feel so well'. The same phenomenon is often seen at parties and discos, where alcohol and loud music induce states of high emotional arousal. If you have ever found someone you met at a party less attractive on second meeting, this may be the reason.

Keeping a good thing going

Maintaining good relationships, whether with friends or sexual partners, is largely a matter of making sure that the processes which first induce liking continue to operate. If someone you used to like or love now seems less likable or lovable, it is usually because one or more of these processes has gone awry. The intermittent nature of meetings with friends means that it is often easier to keep these processes going with them than with partners: we listen to them, compliment them, plan special outings, appreciate them. Married couples, on the other hand, often let months or years pass between outings, and replace praise and compliments with nagging or criticism. Ironically, praise has infinitely more effect on behaviour than criticism—and it keeps liking alive!

More effective	Less effective
Realize that good relationships depend on what you *do*.	Think of relationships in vague, abstract terms.
Create, and make full use of, opportunities to come into regular contact with others.	Expect people to beat a path to your door.
Mix with people who share your attitudes and interests.	Mix with people with whom you have little in common.
Express your opinions and attitudes so that others can recognize similarities with you.	Keep your opinions and attitudes to yourself.
Show interest in others by asking questions.	Answer questions briefly and seldom ask or return them.
Disclose roughly the same amount of personal information to others as they disclose to you.	Say nothing or everything about yourself, regardless of what others reveal.
If you like someone, let them know.	Keep your good opinion of others to yourself.

More successful	Less successful
Don't express liking indiscriminately.	Express good opinions about everyone.
Comment positively on people's less obvious good points.	Comment on good points which are obvious to anyone and everyone.
Give praise only when it is due.	Give praise whether it is deserved or not.
Don't use flattery to influence others.	Rely on flattery to get what you want.

7

Improving self-respect

Good name in man or woman, dear my lord,
Is the immediate jewel of their souls;
Who steals my purse steals trash; 'Tis some-
    thing, nothing;
'Tis mine, 'tis his and has been slave to
    thousands;
But he that filches from me my good name
Robs me of that which not enriches him,
And makes me poor indeed.

WILLIAM SHAKESPEARE (1564–1616)

'Self-respect' is a useful way of talking about that extra confidence which comes from having achieved what you set out to do in the right sort of way. Most people would agree that to achieve success by indirect means or in a concealed fashion is often to lose the enjoyment that goes with success, and often one's self-respect too. When looking for ways to realize personal objectives with other people, then, it is worth looking for paths which maintain or enhance self-respect. Moreover, evidence shows that increasing your self-respect actually improves your social effectiveness!

In general, psychological literature contains no clear definition of the term 'self-respect'. In this book, though, we would like to define it as consisting of two aspects: a sense of mastery, and a sense of morality. Our sense of mastery is composed of a belief that we are in control of things that are important to us. Our sense of morality, on the other hand, demands that our behaviour should not contradict our values or beliefs. The relationship between mastery and morality is not a fixed one, and it is likely to vary widely from individual to individual. Yet in general terms it is possible to talk about ways in which these two aspects of self-respect can be threatened and reinforced.

Threats to mastery

The American psychologist Albert Bandura has observed that we base most of our feelings of mastery on past personal accomplishments. A history of successful performance, he suggests, is likely to breed an expectation of success in future tasks. However, if we fall short of our best performance in particular circumstances, then our sense of mastery is likely to be threatened. John is a businessman who prides himself on his golf score. He practises constantly to shave strokes off his score and has steadily improved his game as a result. One afternoon he is scheduled to play golf with a business associate whose company is about to award John a very lucrative contract. John hears from others in the clubhouse that Martin, his golf partner, plays a poor game of golf but has a terrible temper while playing and is a bad loser. John realizes that he is going to have to let his opponent win: his company needs the contract. In this situation, John's sense of mastery on the golf course is threatened, but he has to weigh that threat against the threat of losing the contract.

This is a very simple example in which the choice is clearcut; moreover John has a degree of freedom to make that choice. But supposing that someone is unemployed and poor, even though he or she wants to work; it might be very difficult to maintain a sense of mastery if confronted with another individual who is rich, powerful and successful. Under these circumstances the person in the weaker position may have to resort to wiles and manipulation in order to have some control over the outcome of the interaction. But the use of such indirect methods of control does not usually enhance the individual's sense of mastery. In *The Marriage of Figaro*, Figaro, a poor barber, finds that his fiancée is desired by her employer, a powerful aristocrat called Count Almaviva. After a series of stratagems, the wily Figaro is able to save his fiancée, frustrate the Count's lustful intentions and maintain his position in the Count's entourage. But at the end of the comedy, the servant is still the servant and the Count is still the master. Historically, women have used indirect persuasion to maintain a measure of control in a world in which direct control was attributed to men by virtue of their role (husband, boss). Such tactics may be effective ('I just let him think he's the boss, then I do what I want') and even admired by others in a similar position ('she's got him twisted around her little finger'). However, one's sense of mastery is unlikely to be increased if it can never be admitted that one has mastery.

Even when disparity of status is not obvious, a sense of mastery can be threatened by a process of slow erosion. Most of us at one time or another have come into contact with an individual who repeatedly demonstrates that he or she does not respect our ideas. When that individual is a spouse or close friend, the effect on our self-respect can be devastating. Remarks like 'You can't really mean that', 'You shouldn't feel that way', 'That's nonsense', or 'Don't be silly' cast doubt upon our belief in our own efficacy. The other person is often unaware of the effect of such statements but, through them, the whole relationship can be put in jeopardy.

Sometimes the effect is more subtle. Janet has noticed that every time she talks with her father she ends up feeling that, as a mother, she is doing everything wrong. She decides to listen carefully to what her father is saying during their next conversation about the children. She discovers that he is constantly questioning her as to her decisions regarding the children: 'Are you sure it's a good idea to leave the children with someone so inexperienced?', 'Aren't they a little young to be up so late?', 'Is that all they're having for lunch?' Little by little Janet's sense of mastery is being eroded. She may decide to stand up to her father the next time she feels her self-respect slipping.

Our own behaviour, as well as that of others, may serve to diminish our belief in our own competence. If we respond in a helpless fashion when difficulties arise and present ourselves as floundering and hopeless, it is not surprising that others treat us as incompetent.

Threats to morality

The morality aspect of self-respect is partly an awareness of our own beliefs and values, and partly a sense that one is behaving in a way which matches up to those values. The system of values we hold helps us select appropriate objectives to work for and indicates acceptable ways in which to get them. Peter places a high value on being successful in his company and, for him, that means getting an important promotion. When promotion time comes round, Peter has been told that he and Mary are being considered for the same job. Peter thinks he will probably not get the promotion since Mary has been with the company longer. Suddenly the opportunity arises for Peter to pass on some confidential information about Mary which, if generally known, would jeopardize her chances of promotion. For a moment Peter is tempted to take advantage of this piece of information but, much as he wants promotion, he also places a high value on being above board in his dealings with other people. He rejects the temptation and accepts that Mary is, after all, likely to get the job.

In this example Peter's objective (the job) and his most effective method of obtaining it (revealing confidential information) are in conflict. He decides that it is more important for him to uphold his belief in himself as a trustworthy person than to attain his objectives dishonestly.

Different values

Like threats to mastery, threats to values can come from our own behaviour or from people and circumstances we encounter. We can act in ways which are inconsistent with our values, or we can do or say nothing in situations where our values would normally demand action.

What happens when someone asks us to approve of their behaviour, even though it goes against our personal standards? Mark and Sam work in an office equipment suppliers. Sam is one of the many workers at the warehouse who regularly takes home ballpoint pens, typing paper and so on for his personal use. Mark strongly disapproves of this. One night Sam asks Mark to help him carry a typewriter which he is 'lending' to his son in order to type up a special piece of schoolwork. Sam also asks Mark to tell the other workers that the typewriter has been sent out for 'cleaning'. Mark resents being implicated, in the first place, in an action of which he disapproves and, in the second place, in having to tell a lie. On the other hand it is important for Mark to have a good working relationship with Sam. Should he keep quiet—or should he report Sam to the supervisor?

A similar dilemma occurs when someone attacks values that are important to us or criticises a person to whom we feel loyal. By remaining quiet, we may be indicating that we agree with the speaker, or that we don't care very much one way or the other. In some sense, by not defending our values or the friends we admire, we are not sticking up for ourselves either. There are certainly times when it is best to keep

102

silence, as when a political speech is being made and someone else has the floor, or when the speaker appears violent and is much larger than we are. But we at least need to be aware of the choice we have made and why we have made it.

Enhancing self-respect

Reinforcing our sense of self-respect requires two approaches: behavioural, to back our sense of mastery, and reflective, a process of finding out what our moral values are, through self-questioning and discussion with other people. There is certainly good evidence to show that, when we perceive ourselves as acting masterfully, we tend to increase our belief in our efficacy. So it may be a good idea to consider finding tasks you know you do well and take a special pride in them. You can then use those feelings of accomplishment to help you tackle another task. You might tell yourself 'I certainly did that job rather well. There is absolutely no reason why I shouldn't do this one just as well.' If you follow this procedure regularly, your belief in your own ability really will rise.

Now let's look at some practical ways of improving your sense of mastery in personal encounters. Remember this does not mean dominating other people, but it should involve care in what you say and how you present yourself to them. In the course of the day, for example, you may receive a compliment on your work, your appearance, or the way you handled a tricky situation. Accepting compliments graciously can help to build your self-respect. Some people find compliments very difficult to accept, perhaps out of the mistaken idea that it is wrong to seem 'big-headed'. Such people get fewer compliments as time goes on. If someone tells you you have handled a difficult situation well, you have a choice: you can say 'Well, I don't know . . . maybe I could have handled it better' or 'Thank you, I appreciate your saying that'. Again, if you present yourself as competent, other people are more likely to have confidence in your abilities. One way of presenting competence to others is to begin sentences with the word 'I'. ('I think we should do this', 'I really like the job you're doing', 'I want you to look this over and tell me what you think.') These kinds of sentences define you as a person with opinions and wishes worth taking seriously. Contrast the above sentences with these: 'Don't you think we should do this?', 'That's a nice job', 'If you're not too busy, could you look at this?'

Choose your environment

Finally there is the question of the environment we find ourselves in. Experiments show that our sense of self-respect can be vitally affected by the quality of the people we normally associate with. It would be hard to maintain a sense of mastery under circumstances where other people are considerably more intelligent, talented or experienced than we are. Selecting an environment in which we do not repeatedly suffer damaging comparison with others may be helpful in increasing our sense of mastery and our respect and liking for ourselves. On the other hand many people stay in situations which they know are very injurious to their self-respect. The socially competent person chooses his or her situations carefully, accepting that sometimes the best course may be to find circum-stances in which success is easier.

Sometimes we cannot change the environment significantly, but we can perhaps alter the way in which we perceive it. For example, it is very easy to get into the habit of brooding upon other people's negative responses, while discounting anything posi-tive they have to say. A simple, but golden, rule is to give equally careful attention to both kinds of responses. Learning to gauge other people's reactions accurately boosts self-confidence and encourages better communication. Over-sensitivity to criticism diminishes our opinion of ourselves.

Enhancing morality

The two most useful approaches in reinforcing our sense of morality are first to identify what our values are, and second, to find opportunities to behave in ways which match those values.

It is not unusual, for example, to be in situations where we are not sure what our values are, or where we appear to hold conflicting values. As a result we find ourselves feeling either unsure or uncomfortable about our decisions or our behaviour. But how do we find out what our values are?

One way is to talk with other people about their values and compare their lives with ours. Another way is to examine our own lives and carefully note our behaviour under conflicting circumstances. We may discover that we have a hierarchy of values, some of which we are willing to sacrifice for the sake of others. We may discover that we have two sets of values, one for a work setting, another for home life. Sometimes we get the impression that our values are there, buried somewhere, and that if only we could get at them we could begin to live by them. This is not always the case. We may have rejected a number of the values that others hold, but have nothing to replace them with. Values *can* be created; they don't have to be the product of a lifetime of experience.

Problems arise when the values we hold are contradictory. Nancy values close friendships and hates to hurt people. Peter is going through a bad time personally and she wants to comfort him, but he is married and his wife is upset at what she imagines to be a developing love affair. As a result of this experience Nancy decides that in future situations in which there is a conflict between helping one person and hurting another, she will choose to avoid hurting others and find ways of helping that don't involve hurting.

Values are not static: they evolve, and they involve a great deal of choice. Like Nancy we may have to decide to emphasize one value rather than another. Or we may choose to apply values more appropriately. Paul is very ambitious and wants to get to the top in a very competitive profession. Yet he has a strong social conscience and believes that one should actively help other people. There is a potential conflict of values which Paul resolves by deciding to limit his attempts to get to the top to strategies which foster co-operation and the good of the greatest number of people. He cannot keep his self-respect by single-mindedly pursuing purely personal interests.

In the light of what we have said so far it is time to summarize what we can do to maintain and enhance our self-respect. On the question of mastery we should concentrate on things that we do well, try to present an impression of competence, and as far as possible leave others in no doubt that we are individuals with our own wishes and opinions. Moreover we should choose our ground, selecting environments where we have at least an even chance of performing well. On the question of values we should try to find out what our values are by talking and comparing them with other people's, and be aware that sometimes we will have to choose between conflicting values.

   Putting all this together needs practice and rehearsal. In fact, for social effectiveness in general, it is a good thing to develop as large a repertoire of social behaviours as possible. From the self-respect point of view greater flexibility allows us to choose whatever strategy seems most appropriate to maintaining relationships with others without violating our basic standards. Having the skills to say No in situations that threaten our values increases our chances of resisting unwanted persuasion. Debbie is a teenager who is often present at parties where drugs are freely used. She is opposed to using them herself and because she is able to say No to them in a firm, clear, yet non-antagonizing way, she is able to go on attending parties, which she enjoys, without jeopardizing her personal values.

As a final tip, we suggest a 'time-out' rule. Often we don't realize that our self-respect has taken a knock until it is too late to do anything about it. If you find yourself in a situation which is not going quite the way you would like, it is worth stepping aside from it for a few minutes and thinking about what is going on. Sometimes this small respite can help us to clarify and evaluate our behaviour.

In general we increase our self-respect when we treat ourselves with respect, as someone who is competent and as someone who is ethical. According to researcher Sandra Bem, when we treat ourselves as worthy of respect we are observing our behaviour towards ourselves, and when we see ourselves treating ourselves with respect, we do indeed become worthy of respect.

8

You
and groups

There can be little liking where there is no
likeness.

AESOP (c. 620–c. 560 BC)

Until now we have concentrated on one-to-one
interactions, since it is usually our relationships with
individuals which most worry us, and most please us.
But we are all members of groups, and so in this
chapter we examine how objective and relationship
effectiveness can be helped or hindered by being one
of a crowd. Most of the processes we've discussed
apply to groups as well as to individuals, but there are
some which are specific to groups, and may help you
not only to decide which groups to join, but also how
to get the most out of them.

In a loose sense, any gathering of people is a group,
but more normally 'group' connotes some shared aim
or loyalty, a political party as distinct from the people
who wait at the bus-stop every morning. There is also
a distinction between groups we are 'forced' to join
(social classes, families, grades at school) and those we
join voluntarily. Some of the processes which operate
within all these groups are the same, but there are
important differences. It might be easier, for example,
to move out of our social class than to resign from a

group we chose to join, but the rules and structures of voluntary groups can be just as rigid and tradition-bound as those obtaining in a tribe or a family. One important difference between voluntary and non-voluntary organizations is that the rules of the latter are rarely written down, rarely available for inspection. Nevertheless, behaviour may be very closely governed by them.

A GROUP   and   AN INDIVIDUAL.

The pressure to conform

The group process which has attracted the most attention from social psychologists is conformity. The term 'conformist' is often used derogatorily, but it applies to all of us. Those we dub 'non-conformist' are still conforming (sometimes rigidly) to the rules of a group. Conformity is neither good nor bad. Yet the world would be an utterly chaotic place without the controlling effects of group pressure on individual behaviour. Indeed, it is impossible to overstate the powerfulness of the pressure to conform, even if the form it takes is called 'rebellion'. Most rebels conform quite rigidly to the norms of rebel groups.

If you join a group, pressure will be exerted on you, explicitly or implicitly, to conform. Knowing this, and knowing how far you are prepared to conform, should enable you to analyse whether membership of a particular group will be rewarding or frustrating. A small number of feminist groups, for example, disapprove of members who form permanent relationships with men; people who join political groups because of specific issues often find that their gross political direction is difficult to support. The choice for the non-conforming member is to rethink or be rejected. Stanley Schachter has shown that, although the non-conformist may not be rejected immediately, the rewards of belonging to a particular group gradually get withdrawn, sometimes to the point of total non-communication (sending someone to Coventry) or humiliation (imposing menial tasks on them). The more cohesive the group, the stronger the commitment expected of its members, the more likely it is to reject its non-conformists.

Non-conformity is, of course, a threat to the group's effectiveness. If members are working towards a common goal—winning an election, improving local amenities, developing a new product—there is more chance of achieving that goal if everyone adopts the same rules and standards. Even two deviating members can be profoundly damaging to group effort and solidarity. Solomon Asch found that people tend to conform about 35 per cent of the time, even if they think group decisions are wrong, *provided the group is unanimous*. In these studies the 'group', in league with the experimenter, was instructed to reach clearly wrong decisions. But if even one member of the 'group' was instructed to dissent from the rest, Asch's volunteers tended to show a lesser degree of conformity. One dissenting voice may be cajoled back into the fold, but two dissenting voices are another matter. This fact has clear implications for group leaders as well as non-conformists.

Who conforms?

There have been a number of studies in social psychology designed to shed light on which individuals in the group are most likely to conform and agree with group decisions. In general, the research suggests that conformity to the group norm is greater under these conditions: when individuals anticipate future interaction with the group, when they are particularly attracted to the group, when they have a somewhat lower status than do other members of the group, and when they do not feel completely accepted by the group. Thus, the individual who is trying to 'break into' a new group is most likely to go along with the members' views, rather than express divergent opinions. It makes sense that, to be identified as a member of a particular group, an individual would attempt to present himself or herself as already similar to the members.

The costs of conformity

Another striking feature of groups is that they tend to absolve their members from individual responsibility. The extent to which this happens, of course, depends on the size and type of group. In general, the larger the group, the stronger the tendency towards 'de-individuation'. Social psychologists suggest that this is because people in large groups feel they lack individual identity.

'Groupthink' is a term that has been coined by psychologist Irvine Janis to describe a situation in which a group decision is made primarily to preserve group cohesiveness, while, at the same time, objectivity and careful analysis of the problem by group members are suspended. Members who engage in groupthink are so concerned about presenting a united, cohesive front that they seem to suspend their good judgement. A strong, autocratic leader is often responsible for groupthink phenomena: group members may be reluctant to examine and discuss views that differ from those of the leader.

Most of the research on de-individuation has been prompted by its role in causing anti-social behaviour. Philip Zimbardo, in a now famous experiment conducted at Stanford University in 1971, assigned the roles of 'prisoner' and 'guard' to a group of male student volunteers, and put them in a simulated prison environment, complete with uniforms, cells and prison rules. The 'guards' quickly became tyrannical and abusive while the 'prisoners' became cowed and submissive. The behaviour of both groups became so extreme that the experiment was stopped after six days. Other research has looked at crowd and riot behaviour and the acts of violence or abuse which people commit when they are members of large groups, acts they would never dream of committing as independent individuals. One reason for this may be that in groups responsibility tends to be diffused, so that both members and outsiders will blame the group rather than an individual for misdemeanours. This process, together with conformity, may also account for the often irrational decisions made by groups and which would not be made by any of their members individually.

The de-individuation process also operates in another way: if a group is credited with good or positive action, the credit belongs to the group, not to any individual in it. This 'spreading' of reward can dampen individual members' enthusiasm for the group's ideals, unless their identification with the group is particularly strong. The lesson here is that if you like recognition for your achievements, you are unlikely to be happy working in a large group.

Achieving objectives by joining a group

Many goals are much easier, or only possible, to achieve through groups. Politicians, for example, willingly lend an ear to large pressure groups, but individual lobbyists seldom get a hearing. Being part of a group also gives us access to information and skills we do not have ourselves. Groups also provide many opportunities for learning by observation, and so help us to generate new behaviours and achieve new goals both within and outside them. Groups also provide rewards and privileges—access to a club or a profession, for example, may be barred unless you are a member of a particular group. The privileges gained by joining a group are, of course, a *quid pro quo* for abiding by certain rules—no conformity, no privileges.

The group is therefore a valuable instrument for gaining certain objectives, and these may be gained with greater certainty by becoming leader of the group. Research has repeatedly shown that leaders have the lion's share of influence: since communication within the group is directed at or channelled through the leader, he or she inevitably wields the most power.

Leadership style

Psychologist Fred Fiedler has suggested that leaders come in two moulds: one is the sort of person whose main concern is to get the job done, the other is mainly concerned with reducing anxiety and increasing satisfaction within the group. Which of these leadership styles is more effective depends on the group and the task in hand: when chaos reigns, or when the relationship between members and leader is good, the 'task-oriented' leader is more successful. When the task is already well defined or when co-operation between members needs improving, the 'group-oriented' leader fares better. Anyone ambitious to become a leader should consider what style he or she should adopt, taking into account the nature of the group and the task involved. Competence and likability do not necessarily qualify one for leadership. Moreover, leaders are not generally the best-liked members of groups. It may therefore be difficult to combine objective and relationship effectiveness if you are top dog.

A leadership characteristic repeatedly found by researchers is that leaders like to talk—the so-called

Big Mouth theory of leadership! In one study, both the quantity and quality of people's verbal contributions to group discussions were manipulated. The quality of what was said had little effect on whether the person was seen as a leader; it was quantity which counted. An interesting study lends further support to the Big Mouth theory of leadership. Groups of four people each were brought together to discuss the merits of different paintings. One of the subjects, a confederate, was actually working with the experimenter and was introduced into the groups as either an expert or a non-expert. Then, during group discussions about the paintings, the confederate was either the most talkative member or one of the least talkative members.

Following the discussions, group members were asked to nominate the leader of the group and to identify the person who had had the most influence on the group discussions about the paintings. The 'expert' was overwhelmingly identified as the leader of the groups, whether or not she was talkative. However, talking a lot or a little made a critical difference in the case of the non-expert: the talkative non-expert was more often nominated as the leader of the group and identified as guiding group discussions than was the non-expert who talked very little. The talkative non-expert was perceived in much the same way as the expert in terms of guiding discussion and having the best ideas. In this case, the old adage about keeping your mouth shut when you don't know anything doesn't seem to be the best advice if your goal is to influence others and to be seen as a leader.

Forming relationships through groups

Being liked may not be compatible with being a leader, but most people join groups with aims other than leadership. One of the most potent reasons for joining groups is simply to meet others. Subconsciously, we know that friendships are most likely to arise from regular contact with like-minded people. Of course, not all groups meet regularly or often, a fact which may be obvious ('meetings are held twice a year') or sometimes unstated. Some 'friendship' groups expect new members, after an initial get-together, to initiate contact amongst themselves, which may make good sense administratively, but is not good psychology— people who join such groups often find it very difficult to make contacts on their own initiative.

Shared aims and attitudes

One major advantage of groups is that they give us the opportunity to mix with people who are in some way similar to us. Friendships blossom in groups based on shared attitudes and values, or on interests which imply other attitudes—people who enjoy sport or ancient history are likely to have other attitudes in common. But it may be more difficult to make friends in groups based on some other characteristic, such as age, sex, or occupation; in this case the larger the group the greater the chance of finding people who share your values. Imagine, for instance, a small local club for divorced people or for single parents—the people in it may have so little in common other than their singleness that meetings become a strain rather than a pleasure.

Generally, people appear more attractive to one another if they are co-operating rather than compet-ing. Co-operation is conducive to liking. It therefore follows that groups which have co-operative aims— mutual help, or simply having a good time—are more likely to breed friendships than competitive groups in which members are always pitting their skills against one another.

Group geography

Unfortunately, there has been very little research on 'socializing' in groups, but it is usually assumed that the same verbal and non-verbal skills and rules apply as in one-to-one interactions. But one point which becomes especially important in group settings is the effect of seating arrangements on communications. We know that the width of a table or the orientation of speakers in relation to each other can make conversation more or less difficult. Given a choice, people prefer to talk across a space which does not require them to raise their voice or lean too much in the other person's direction—lovers being the obvious exception to this! We also prefer to look at, but not directly at, each other and therefore orient ourselves towards but at an angle to each other, unless the seating arrangements demand that we sit directly opposite.

In groups the process is even more complex, because speakers must orient themselves in relation to more than one person. Here, in general, we tend to address remarks to those opposite rather than beside us—obviously, it is less awkward than constantly turning our heads. The alternative is to turn the whole body to one side, but this may exclude the person opposite! But if this person is some distance away, we tend to address most of our remarks sideways—again, the alternative would be to exclude the person to one side by leaning towards the 'opposite' speaker. Our relationship to other people in the group is also a crucial factor: if two people who know each other well are seated side by side, a third person will tend to get ignored, but if the third person is sitting between them, he or she will probably be drawn into the conversation, it being considered rude to 'talk across' people. If you ever feel 'left out' at a social gathering, look carefully at the seating or standing arrangements. It might not be your social skills which are to blame, simply that the human geography is discouraging you from using them.

9

When in Rome . . .

Nothing seems at first sight less important than the outward form of human actions, yet there is nothing upon which men set more store: they grow used to everything except to living in a society which has not their own manners.

ALEXIS DE TOCQUEVILLE (1805–1859)

We are so familiar with the patterns of behaviour, acceptable in our own culture, that it can be difficult to appreciate how strange or alarming they seem to people from other cultures. 'Culture' has been defined by some anthropologists as 'that part of the human environment determined by people rather than geography'. Others suggest a slightly narrower meaning: culture is a set of beliefs common to any group. According to the latter definition, every family constitutes a separate culture. To a certain extent every family does, but for our purposes the family is too narrow a unit in which to talk meaningfully about general social behaviour, so we take the wider perspective and focus on cultures as groups of people who are very different in terms of language, heritage and behaviour. This is not to suggest that there is no overlap in social behaviour between cultures nor wide individual differences within them—there are extremely emotional English people and very reserved Italians. On the whole, however, broad patterns of behaviour are discernible which are different from group to group.

The basics of social behaviour are identical throughout the world. Everyone smiles, talks, laughs, frowns, touches, stands close or apart. The differences reside in the complex rules which surround the display of these behaviours. Learning social behaviour does not only involve learning *what* to do (how to start a conversation, for instance) but *when* and *with whom* to do it. These rules are so much a part of our lives that we are often unaware of them until someone breaks them—imagine a complete stranger coming to sit beside you on a bus when all the other seats are empty. When we observe a particular display of social behaviour, we almost invariably interpret it in terms of our own cultural rules, partly of course because we are not familiar with any others. These two factors, display and interpretation, are the basic currency of all social encounters. The difficulties which arise in interpreting the 'displays' of members of our own culture are minor compared with the potential for misunderstanding inherent in encounters between members of different cultures.

Cultural differences

It would be literally impossible to list all the differences in behaviour patterns which exist among members of different cultures. But, even if we could, the act of listing them might imply, wrongly, that such patterns are 'fixed'. We therefore give some general examples of cultural variations in universal behaviours and then show how they are used in greeting and parting rituals.

Eye contact

Looking another person in the eye is one of the basic ingredients of most social encounters, but an elaborate set of rules governs when and how long we look. An extensive study of cultural differences in eye gaze found that Arabs, Latin Americans and Southern Europeans focus their gaze on the eyes or face of their conversational partner; Asians, Indians, Pakistanis and Northern Europeans, however, tend to show 'peripheral' gaze (they look towards but not directly at the other person's face) or no gaze (they look at the floor or into space). Interestingly, no relationship between gaze behaviour and time spent in a foreign country was found, and so it was concluded that eye contact habits are deeply ingrained. Put an English-man and an Arab together, and the Englishman might feel very uncomfortable about his companion's fixed gaze, while the Arab might feel very insulted at having his gaze avoided.

Personal space

We all have around us a 'space' which we permit others to enter only under certain well-defined conditions. If these complex rules are broken, we become extremely uncomfortable and do everything possible to re-establish a comfortable distance. In his book, *The Hidden Dimension*, E.T. Hall reported that Americans behave as if there were four zones of personal space, depending on the relationship of the two people interacting. Intimate distance is less than 18 inches, personal distance between 18 inches and 4 feet, social distance between 4 and 12 feet, and public distance between 12 and 25 feet. These distances are relatively large and they vary considerably across cultures. Germans, for example, seem to need even more space than Americans, who are similar to the English and the Swedes. In contrast, Arabs and Southern Europeans usually interact at much closer distances. Desmond Morris has described our inter-personal frontiers as being at fingertip, wrist or elbow distance, and remarks on the well-known embassy reception phenomenon of 'fingertip' guests gradually edging across the room to re-establish this distance between themselves and 'elbow' guests until, having lost the battle, they end up pinned to the wall!

SOCIAL DISTANCE

Touch

Intuitively one would expect patterns of touch to be related to personal distance preferences, and this is indeed the case. A study, consisting of one-hour observation sessions in cafés in various parts of the world, found that the hourly touch rate between Puerto Ricans was 180, between the French 110, between Americans 2 and between the English none! Another striking finding by the same researcher was that in highly 'tactile' cultures, men touched each other as often as opposite sex pairs touched. In low tactile cultures, almost all touching is between females or between companions of the opposite sex.

The power of touch in a culture where it is not used freely was shown in a study by Fischer and his colleagues. They trained a library clerk to brush the

TOUCHING.

hands of some students but not others when they returned their library cards. The students were then approached and asked to fill in a rating scale, saying what they thought of the library's facilities and of the staff. Those who had been touched by the librarian tended to give more positive ratings. This result is particularly interesting given the very fleeting nature of the physical contact involved—in fact, many of the students had no conscious recollection of having been touched. It is possible, of course, that casual touching might have had a different effect on people from a highly tactile culture.

Greetings and partings

When social behaviours follow a set sequence in certain circumstances, they take on the character of ritual. Two of the most important rituals in any society are those which signal the beginning and end of a social encounter. Stop for a moment and count the number of ways in which you perform these rituals, and then the number of ways in which other people of the same culture perform them. We do not greet friends or lovers in the same way as acquaintances, nor do we greet the same people in the same way in different situations, for example when we have not seen them for a long time, or meet them at a party, or at work, or in the street, or at a funeral. So in scrutinizing cross-cultural patterns of greetings and partings, we also have to take account of the relationships between people and the circumstances in which they meet. We talk only about greetings here, because partings are really their mirror-image, involving the same rituals.

Is this goodbye?

GREETINGS and PARTINGS.

Because greetings involve gaze, proximity and touch, it is not surprising to find that cultural differences in greetings reflect differences in the display of these behaviours. Members of all cultures seem to share 'distant' greetings, made up of head movements, smiles and some kind of wave. It is when we come within touching or speaking distance that situational and cultural diversity begin to appear. In Britain and America, for example, the handshake is usually reserved for first meetings, formal occasions or occasions when some kind of extra acknowledgement seems warranted (this happens mostly among men). Similarly a full embrace tends to occur only between very close friends, family members or intimates and even then only when emotions run high. For less emotional occasions or meetings with less well-known people, the full embrace appears in an abbreviated form, such as grasping the arms and kissing, or pretending to kiss, the cheek. It is often very noticeable that both parties in these semi-embraces are very concerned not to overdo things, not to turn a relaxed moment into a tense and artificial one.

In contrast, people from 'tactile' countries are less inhibited about their greetings. In much of Europe, for example, the handshake is a very informal greeting, and is used extensively among family and friends in much the same way as Americans use the greeting 'Hi'—which can be extremely disconcerting for people used to shaking hands only with new acquaintances. Similarly, the embrace is more often used as a form of greeting between men, as well as between women and opposite sex pairs.

Generally, people are quick to adopt the greeting patterns of the cultures they visit—they oil the wheels of subsequent interaction. If a greeting, which signifies the beginning of a social exchange, does not go well, the rest of the encounter will suffer. A common exception to this rule is when a host, or a host country, to show deference and respect to a visitor, displays the visitor's greeting pattern, even though this makes the visitor feel extremely uncomfortable. Heads of state visiting foreign countries are greeted with their own national anthem, their national flag and speeches in their own language . . . For most of us, however, if we want to be as effective abroad as at home, the rule must be 'When in Rome . . .'

Differences within differences

Because inter-cultural diversity in the display of social behaviour is so marked, we sometimes forget that even within the same culture there are many 'sub-cultures' with distinct and different patterns of behaviour.

Four sub-cultures which immediately spring to mind are those defined by age, racial group, social class and gender. When we consider that each of us is a member of all four categories simultaneously (teenage, Polish, middle class and male, or middle aged, Welsh, working class and female), the picture gets very complicated indeed. In psychological research on variations in social behaviour within a culture, comparisons have usually been made be-

WOMEN LOOK AT MEN MORE THAN MEN DO . . . .

tween males and females, and even then not very often. Reliable information on sub-cultural differences is therefore fairly scanty.

It seems to be the rule that women look at their conversational partners more than men do, both when talking and listening. This may be related to the suggestion, reported in Chapter 3, that women are more concerned than men about what people think of them. Looking frequently at one's interlocutor provides valuable feedback. On the other hand, this sex difference in eye gaze seems to emerge early in life: Jerome Kagan and Michael Lewis found that even six-month-old girls paid more attention to human faces than boys of the same age. This could, however, be part of a more general early sex difference in 'exploratory' behaviour. Nevertheless, further research suggests that the first theory is correct as far as adult women are concerned: those with high 'need affiliation' (those eager to please and be liked by others) look much more at their conversational partners than women who care rather less about people's good opinion.

Differences have also been found in the personal space preferences of men and women. Women stand closer to and more directly facing other women than men do when they are talking to men. Women also seem to get less upset by being in crowded conditions which force them into contact with other women. In an experimental crowding situation with same-sex groups, women actually became more relaxed while men became increasingly uncomfortable. When the researchers erected barriers between the crowded participants, the men immediately relaxed, whereas the women showed no reaction.

These results, of course, do not tell us anything about how these differences in social behaviour are related to effectiveness. There has, in fact, been very little research in this area, but studies on group communication do provide some clues. We have seen that groups can be instrumental in obtaining personal objectives, provided the other members of the group can be persuaded to go along with one's ideas. In group settings, women have been found to be less concerned with problem-solving and persuasion than with supporting what others have said. Women in mixed-sex groups also talk less than the men, and make fewer contributions directly related to the problem to be solved. Applying the Big Mouth theory of leadership, then, men automatically have more influence on group decisions than women. But the question whether women would be more influential if only they talked more remains unanswered.

Because very little research has been done in this area, we can only speculate about sub-cultural differences in social effectiveness. In the absence of respectable evidence, then, we must rely on our own observations and come to our own conclusions, based on what we see working for others!

10

Putting it all together

As is our confidence, so is our capacity.

WILLIAM HAZLITT (1778–1830)

It is probably a safe assumption that all of us could benefit from some improvement in our social skills. Given the complexity and variety of the skills we use in social interactions, this is not surprising. The aim of this chapter is to help readers recognize situations in which self-change is proper and practical, and situations in which no amount of self-change will bring about the desired result. Realism is the key to all analysis and effort at change. There are situations in which even the most skilled behaviour is irrelevant. Having realistically examined both your problem and your social skills, you should be able to assess whether it is worth trying to change.

Don't be vague

It is a truism that unless one has a detailed idea of what a problem is, it is difficult if not impossible to solve it. People who seek therapy are often very sure that they know what their problem is: 'I'm no good with people', they say, or 'Everyone seems so unfriendly', or 'People never listen to me when I complain'. Assessments such as this are about as helpful as saying to a motor mechanic: 'The engine's making a funny noise' or 'The car won't start'.

The purpose of a 'social' assessment is to gather very specific information about behaviour and the situations in which it happens. A skilled therapist will go through the same procedure (sometimes called situational analysis) with clients, the object being not only to define the problem in specific (behavioural) terms, but also to find out how it varies from situation to situation. The therapist can then begin to look for differences between troublesome and trouble-free situations, differences which are often valuable pointers to the cause of the client's problem. This may sound straightforward, but is something that people find very difficult to do for themselves. One of the most taxing tasks for the therapist is to encourage clients away from vague, general descriptions of themselves and into the specifics of their problem. Since this chapter is mainly concerned with self-analysis, the remarks which follow are designed to help the reader be specific about his or her problem.

Information gathering

One useful way to think about social assessment is to see it as a process of gathering enough information to answer the question: *What is causing the problem—your behaviour, the situation, or both?* This is a chicken-and-egg question, because behaviour forms part of any situation and if behaviour changes, the situation changes. There are, however, some wider situations which exist more or less independently of personal behaviour—those created by the legal, educational or economic system, for example. Assuming that the answer to the question is 'both', as it often is, here are some guidelines which might help you pin down the major cause of your problem:

(a) Review the problem interaction and ask yourself: Could I have behaved more effectively? Writing things down may help you to get your ideas straight, as well as remind you of things you did not notice at the time.

(b) Try consciously to keep track of your behaviour in similar situations, either as they happen or as soon as possible afterwards. If you come to the conclusion that you usually handle such situations well and behave in a similar fashion in the specific problem situation, then the problem situation must be different in some significant way. Either you need new skills for that particular situation, or the situation is unworkable given the goals you have in mind.

(c) Compare yourself with other people in similar situations. Do they fare better or worse than you? Those who achieve more than you do may be different from you in important respects—they may be richer, a lot more talented, or have friends in high places. But watching or reading about others is not always a reliable means of judging whether they are effective, because people often try to hide their ineffectiveness. This is particularly true when failure is stigmatized, as it is in sexual problems, or being 'inadequate' as a wife or mother. The media, especially advertising, also tend to project an inaccurate picture of what people actually achieve—everyone is shown as skilled, competent, effective. A more realistic picture of what people *do* achieve emerges by talking to them. And the bonus of talking to people is that they usually provide you with feedback about your behaviour. A friend or other observer may be able to tell you something it might take you months to see for yourself. If in their honest opinion your behaviour in the problem situations, and in similar situations, is as skilled as can be reasonably expected, you should probably focus on changing the situation.

(d) Try different approaches. New ideas can emerge from reviewing hitherto unsuccessful behaviour, from friends' suggestions, and from the points made in Chapters 5 and 6. If none of them work, then the situation is probably unworkable. There are no rules about when to stop trying. But if you cannot generate new behaviours, or the goal does not seem worth the effort, then it is probably time to stop.

How do you put things right?

Failing in important social situations can be very damaging to one's confidence and self-esteem, and if you have already tried to make changes and failed you are not likely to want to try again. Albert Bandura has suggested that 'self-efficacy', the feeling that one's efforts will be rewarded, constitutes the impetus and incentive behind a lot of human behaviour. But self-efficacy cannot be conjured out of thin air: it comes from actually succeeding, and succeeding often enough to feel confident about being effective in the future. This is a classic Catch 22 situation—unless you think you will succeed you won't try, and unless you try you cannot possibly succeed. Perhaps it is just as well that feelings of self-efficacy can be fostered in other ways, for example, by applying strategies based on the years of research by social psychologists! The methods we discuss below and in the next chapter have proved successful with many people. If you examine your past efforts to change and compare them with the methods we suggest, you may see why things did not work out and muster the confidence and optimism to try again.

It is very important to realize that social skills are not acquired by birth, osmosis, good intentions, talking about them, telling yourself to shape up or just hoping things will improve. They are acquired through learning and practice. If you lack an important skill, it is not because you are stupid or unlikable or a social misfit, but because you have not had the necessary learning experience. Learning being such a complex business, people often give up if they do not get instant results. But would you cancel piano lessons if you couldn't play like Rubinstein after a month?

Strategy

If you decide that your behaviour is the problem, what do you do? The first step is to work out exactly what you are doing wrong. This is easier said than done—you may not be aware of the skills involved in a particular interaction and, even if you are, it is difficult to 'watch' yourself. This is why watching other people deploy their social skills, successfully and unsuccessfully, is so instructive. Chapters 4, 5 and 6 outline many of the skills needed to achieve material and relationship goals. But knowing about these skills is not enough. You must also know whether or not you are using them. A person who neither knows which skills are required nor whether he or she is using them is inevitably vague about the problem, and therefore ill-equipped to do anything about it. A social skills therapist often uses audio or video playback of interactions during therapy sessions to provide clients with feedback. You can always use audio and video at home, of course, but verbal feedback from friends often works just as well. Specifically, ask a friend to tell you when you begin to look bored, or ask too many questions.

An alternative strategy is to specify the skills which seem to 'work' in a particular situation—using information either from previous chapters or from observation of people who seem skilled—and to observe yourself very closely to find out whether or not you are applying these skills. This is easier said than done, but quite feasible as long as you decide in advance which situations you will monitor and which behaviours you will 'observe'. For example, you might set yourself the task of observing how you greet visitors to your home or how you react to compliments, and at first looking only at your verbal behaviour. Obviously, this is going to result in temporary self-consciousness, but this is surely worthwhile in the long run.

One valuable piece of information which clients often discover during this sort of analysis is that they are 'punishing' people who approach them, for

131

example by greeting visitors with tales of woe, or denying that compliments are deserved, or simply not listening.

Lack of skills or misuse of skills?

Let us suppose that you have found out what you are doing wrong in a particular situation. The next step is

Hello - nice to see you..
What a day I've had..
first the boiler burst and then
my ex-wife rang up and
screamed at me - and then
I BURNT the dinner and you're
half an hour late...

to work out whether the cause is the lack of a particular skill, or whether existing skills are being inhibited by negative thinking ('I won't know what to say'), emotional arousal or, more usually, both. If you interact successfully when you are calm or don't care about the outcome (for example, when you are with family and friends, or when you are being interviewed for a job you don't really want), then you probably have the necessary skills and your task is to 'disinhibit' these in the problem situation. If things don't go well even when you are relaxed and putting your best foot forward, the problem is more likely to be a lack of social skill—this is especially true of situations you have little experience of.

As we have seen, three things can inhibit us from using existing skills: emotions, negative thinking and automatic behaviour. Those emotions most likely to interfere with effective behaviour are anger and anxiety. We have described how 'emotion' consists of physiological arousal and a cognitive label, and that it is possible to learn to control arousal consciously, thus reducing the 'emotion'. The technique which therapists most often use to control arousal is 'relaxation training'. You can teach yourself to relax, of course—there are many tapes and instruction books on the market—but formal relaxation classes often give better results. Relaxing properly is a fairly complex skill and best learned with a teacher.

Beliefs and attitudes: are they valid?

Reducing inhibitions by altering one's way of thinking can be difficult, partly because one is usually talking about strongly-held beliefs and attitudes (not necessarily derived from first-hand experience), which are only likely to change *after* alternative beliefs have led to greater satisfaction, and not before. There are, however, two good reasons for closely examining one's beliefs and assumptions. First, many of our thought processes are so automatic that we may never have clarified them before or even been aware of their existence—obviously, beliefs cannot be analysed or refuted if they have not been acknowledged. Second, these beliefs may be based not on personal experience, but on faulty information (who *says* people will not like you unless you talk a lot?). Look at Ellis's list of irrational beliefs in Chapter 3 and try to relate some of them to situations you find difficult. Do you, for example, think you will be rejected if you ask someone for a date? Rejection may be a possibility, but does rejection mean that you are fundamentally unlovable? Do you know others who have been rejected? Are they unlovable? Have you ever rejected someone yourself? If you have, why did you, and how much did it have to do with the other person? One could go on for ever . . . The point is this: at least test whether your negative beliefs have a foundation in reality. If they don't, they should be discarded; they are unlikely to further the social goals you have in mind. Try operating for a while with an opposite and positive set of beliefs. It works.

Guarding against automatic behaviour

The third inhibiting factor—automatic behaviour which slips out at inappropriate moments—can be controlled, with some effort at first, and then with greater ease. The exact moment at which the automatic behaviour occurs must be pinpointed (do you always talk too much when you first meet people? or only when you have had a drink or two?). Then, knowing that such moments are imminent, one can take steps to forestall the automatic behaviour. The problem is to know when danger is looming.

This is how one of the authors of this book solved it for a particular client. Philip M. had the habit of talking incessantly to the people with whom he shared an office, making it impossible for them to get on with their work; since he did a lot of his talking from a vantage point near the coffee machine, he clearly needed an early-warning system which operated the moment he left his desk to go to the coffee machine. The solution was simple and worked beautifully—he put a bunch of paper clips in his shoes each morning when he got to his desk, so that when he stood up the clips pinched and reminded him that he was on the way to the coffee machine and to disturbing everybody! A more general solution to an automatic behaviour might be to ask a sympathetic friend or partner to alert you with an agreed signal as soon as the warning signs appear.

On the whole, you have a better chance of reducing inhibitions to effective social behaviour by combining all three techniques—relaxation, revised thinking, and early warnings of automatic behaviour—than by using just one, but a great deal of practice and perseverance is required. You are unlearning things which it took you a long while to acquire in the first place.

Learning new behaviour in safe environments

Social skills are learned in the same way as any other skill. Having discovered what it is you are doing wrong (re-read Chapters 4, 5 and 6) and worked out what behaviour changes would achieve the outcomes you want, embark on these changes step by step—your best teachers at school were probably those who took you through new material step by step, they did not expect you to learn everything at once. If, for example, an honest and sympathetic friend tells you that your posture is tense, that you don't smile enough and that you don't look at people when they talk to you, then choose just one of these behaviours and work on it. Watch how other people sit or smile or gaze, and practise the new, improved behaviour in situations where you feel most relaxed. At first, you will probably feel more awkward than ever, but gradually the behaviour will become more automatic.

Social skills therapists create 'safe' situations by using 'role-play'. Some experts on improving assertive behaviour advise practising verbal techniques with a tape recorder. But it is important not to be too critical of yourself—even very small improvements should be encouraged. Other safe environments might be at home with friends or family, or in a group of people with similar problems. Always, the important thing is to get feedback about your efforts, since this provides both guidance and positive reinforcement. Sometimes feedback is quite unsolicited—when someone complies with a request, and seems pleased to do so, showing that you have successfully exerted influence *and* maintained a good relationship—but at other times we must actively seek it.

Not only should new skills be tried out in safe environments first, they should be applied to situations which are easy at first and get progressively more challenging. It is surprising how often clients who see a professional therapist choose to tackle the most difficult situations first, perhaps mistakenly seeing them as a challenge. These same people would never consider the racing track the best place to try out their newly-acquired driving skills! One way to gauge the difficulty of a social situation is to analyse it in terms of similarities to, and differences from, other situations in which you have been effective. This sort of analysis requires SJS skills—sensitivity, judgement and self-regulation—but the more you practise assessing social interactions and thinking through alternative courses of action, the more effective you will become. As new situations become more familiar, effective behaviour becomes more automatic. It is when one blindly applies well-learned behaviours to new and possibly very diverse situations that one is most likely to go wrong.

Identifying 'no-win' situations

If, on the other hand, you decide that the basis of your problem is an unworkable situation (see the section on choice, pages 57–58) you then have to work out which aspect of the situation is blocking you and whether you can do anything about it. Remember, 'no-win' situations often arise from discrepancies in social power, where one party, which could be an organization, controls most of the important resources—jobs, housing, affection, and so on. But the weaker parties in such situations often give up prematurely, because

136

they have not analysed the power relationship accurately—they may be unaware, for example, of the range of consumer and employment laws which can give them power over large organizations. Also, low-power people are by definition not accustomed to, and therefore not very skilled at, dealing with high-power, and sometimes very arrogant, people. The low-power person also tends, because of his or her position in the hierarchy, to be insecure—often the situation is blamed, very conveniently, for shortcomings of a personal nature. What we are saying, therefore, is that interpersonal knowledge and skills are not only tools for self-change, but for situation-changing as well.

However, deciding in advance that a situation is unworkable is not only bad detective work, but also self-defeating. Only when you have analysed the situation accurately, gained information about how others cope with similar situations, and tried to acquire some new skills and still failed to change things should your verdict be 'no win'.

The point at which you decide to stop trying will, of course, depend on how important your goal is—recovering a small sum overpaid to the telephone company may not be worth much effort, but saving a marriage may be worth every ounce of energy and perseverance over a long period.

If, having read this chapter, you feel that your particular problem would yield more quickly and surely to professional help, then read the next chapter. Some of the analyses and techniques used by qualified social skills therapists have some application in a self-help context. Until about 15 years ago, the extent and influence of social skills deficits was largely unrecognized. Today it is estimated that one in ten quite normal adults feels significantly hampered by some aspect of his or her social behaviour. There is therefore nothing abnormal about seeking professional help.

11

Professional help

He who would learn to fly one day must first
stand and walk and run and climb and dance:
one cannot fly into flying.

FRIEDRICH NIETZSCHE (1844–1900)

What do you do if, no matter how hard you try, you
cannot make headway with a social problem? Some
people have trouble getting on with almost everyone,
but most people's troubles are limited to one or two
areas. Perhaps the problem is the opposite sex—you
cannot find anyone to date, and when you do, the
other person does not find you as interesting as you
find them. Perhaps the problem is assertion—you just
cannot seem to stand up for yourself and express your
opinions and preferences. Perhaps things are difficult
at work—you lack confidence in front of others or
cannot get along with people above or below you in
the hierarchy. Let's assume you have read some
self-help books and talked with friends, and that you
are still having great difficulty. You know you are
getting less than you want and need from other
people, and you are getting more and more depressed. You decide to seek professional help.

A matter of choice

A very obvious first question, when you decide to seek professional help, is: What sort of help? There are all sorts of professionals offering to help their fellow human beings. Individuals, groups, universities and schools, private and public agencies and businesses, clinics and hospitals—all offer training or therapy designed, either directly or indirectly, to help individuals derive more pleasure and satisfaction from their social encounters.

Generally the sort of help offered can be divided into three categories: (a) growth and encounter groups (EST, sensitivity groups, T-groups) which offer organized experiences intended to enhance your personal awareness; (b) classes which teach one or more specified social skills (assertion, heterosexual skills, personnel management); (c) individual, couples or group therapy with a professional therapist.

Growth groups

The number and variety of growth groups wax and wane with time. Generally such groups offer some form of structured experience, use the group as an environment for growth and learning, and provide participants with feedback and emotional support.

Groups can vary enormously, depending on the philosophy of the person or organization offering the group experience. They vary in size (as small as six to ten people to as large as several hundred); in the structure of the experience offered (sticking to a tight agenda or to almost none at all); in leadership style (trainer- or therapist-led to member-led); in intensity (a few hours a week or month to marathon sessions lasting several days); and in the follow-up offered (from none at all to regular reunions).

Most growth groups do not focus explicitly on increasing members' social skills. It is simply assumed that participants will get out of the group whatever it is they want from the group. Although growth groups are often described as educational (or psycho-educational) the content of the education is usually not stated. Simply by virtue of the collective experience participants have the opportunity to increase their awareness of others and of themselves during social interactions.

How successful are growth groups?

Unfortunately the success of growth groups in helping people to improve their social skills and increase satisfaction with their social activities is unknown since only a limited number of outcome studies have been done and their results are difficult to interpret.

Naturally enough, the organizations which run such groups and, very frequently, satisfied customers give persuasive testimonials, but there are a number of factors which make reliance on such testimonials inadvisable.

First, we do not know how many individuals drop out of growth groups or how many are made more rather than less unhappy by attending them. Second, those who run such groups are likely to be biased in their opinions. Third, satisfied customers may feel very good for a short while after a group experience, but there may be no change in their social skills level—benefits may not last long after the 'glow' of the group wears off. Fourth, without a control group of people who *believe* they are going to be helped by a growth group, even though the group is not helpful in practice, we cannot really tell whether reported change is the result of the group experience or the result of *belief* in the efficacy of the group experience. Fifth, without a comparison group of individuals who want group training but do not receive it, how can we be sure that improvement would not have taken place in any case? Perhaps only people on the verge of changing, with or without training, are motivated to sign up for, pay for, and take part in a growth group.

Social skills classes

Courses explicitly designed to teach particular social skills are offered by various universities, mental health clinics, private organizations and individuals. They cover such specifics as assertion training, heterosexual skills, winning friends and influencing people, public speaking, the art of making conversation, etiquette, negotiating and bargaining, and a host of other skills. As with growth groups these courses are described as educational. As a rule they are conducted in groups, require one or two hours a week for up to eight weeks, and are led by an instructor.

In a well-run class the instructor will provide a method of self-assessment so that class members can chart their progress and judge whether, at the end of the course, they have improved. Classes are usually a blend of lecturing and modelling by the instructor, discussion by the whole class, and role-playing practice sessions. The instructor provides reading materials or recommends textbooks. Generally class members are expected to practise their new skills between classes, keep a record of their progress, and report problems and progress back to the class. Both the instructor and the class give feedback and encouragement.

Although there has been very little research on the effectiveness of courses like these, there has been a good deal of research on the methods which most instructors use. Generally, there is substantial evidence that individuals can improve their social skills in a number of areas by guided practice, both in the classroom and in the real world, by receiving competent instruction, observing models engaging in effective behaviour, and receiving feedback and positive encouragement on their own behaviour.

Individual or group therapy

There is no single definition of counselling or therapy. In very general terms, it is a relationship in which one person enlists the professional assistance of another for the purpose of bringing about changes in feelings, thoughts, attitudes, and/or overt behaviour. The task of the therapist, therefore, is to help individuals assess how they want or need to change and then to help them accomplish those changes. How the therapist goes about assisting the client will depend upon his or her training and theoretical orientation. This will affect his or her style, focus, and the methods and techniques used in therapy. A good therapist will make every effort to modify therapeutic techniques to fit the style and needs of the individual client. Thus, clients who would best benefit from a group might be placed in group therapy, those who would benefit from a structured, teaching style of therapy would receive more instruction and advice, and those who do best by just talking and exploring their own behaviour, feelings, and thoughts, would receive more unstructured therapy in which the therapist gives feedback and suggestions but little structure.

Almost all therapies give considerable attention to the client's interpersonal relationships and behaviour. Generally, the types of therapy available fall into three categories: (a) insight-oriented therapies, (b) action-oriented therapies, and (c) drug-oriented therapies.

In insight therapies, client and therapist spend the session discussing the client's current and past behaviours, thoughts, and feelings with the goal of achieving more insight and perspective into what the client is doing, feeling and thinking, and into the motives influencing these activities. The idea here is that, if you can gain insight into your own behaviour, you can change it for the better. In addition, the relationship with the therapist is an opportunity for you to examine your style of relating to people and learn more productive ways of interacting.

The most well-known action-oriented therapies are the behaviour therapies. The behavioural approach assumes that while insight into the what and why of behaviour may be critically important, explicit focused re-learning in the real world is also important.

The behavioural approach to therapy is very similar to the approach in classes on social skills. Namely, there is likely to be an emphasis on instruction, in-session practice, practice between sessions in the real world, charting or otherwise monitoring progress, feedback and encouragement from the therapist. The difference between behaviour therapy and class sessions is that the therapy is individually designed and based on extensive, individual assessment by both the therapist and the client. Thus, therapy may focus on re-learning if the problem is a skill deficit, on removing interfering thoughts or reducing extreme emotional responses if the problem is response inhibition, or examining motives and clarifying values if the problem is a result of choosing to be ineffective in a particular area.

Drug therapies are very rarely used to enhance social skills. The exception is when interpersonal problems are the result of severe psychosis or deep depression. In either case, medication might be prescribed to reduce the psychosis or lift the depression. However, it should be noted that the effect of the drug is on the psychosis and depression, not on overt behaviour *per se*. If the individual has never learned social skills, it is not possible to create skills and interpersonal effectiveness by chemical intervention.

Most therapists will want to see you weekly, usually for one-hour sessions. The number of sessions is usually individually negotiated. The benefits of insight-oriented therapies in improving social skills and interpersonal satisfaction have not been well tested. Although there have been many research studies on these treatments, most studies have not directly measured whether the person actually improves behaviourally and interpersonally. Many studies, however, have shown that people generally report feeling better after insight therapy. In contrast, there have been numerous studies on interpersonal skill training done by the behaviour therapists. As noted above, results have indicated that for many people, a combination of instruction, practice, feedback and encouragement, and modelling of successful behaviours, can be beneficial in improving interpersonal skills. It is not yet clear how well these gains are maintained or how well skills learned in one area generalize to other areas.

Choosing between growth groups, classes and therapy

How do you choose the method which will help you most? With growth groups you must realize that the central goal is not explicitly to improve social skills. Though you might benefit from such a group, the benefits may be in other areas. If your primary aim is to improve your interpersonal skills and derive more pleasure from your social encounters, you should ask the leader or organizer of the group whether social skills will be focused on and whether you can expect improvement in this area. Growth groups certainly provide social experiences, but they do not normally provide instruction, advice and material directly relevant to social behaviour. So you must be prepared to integrate the group experiences with the rest of your experiences yourself. Often growth groups create experiences that arouse strong emotions, and some groups discourage you from dropping out if you find those experiences distressing. If you feel under considerable stress already, or feel depressed, vulnerable or unstable, a growth group is probably not a good idea.

Social skills classes of some sort are generally offered in most large cities. If they are offered near you, if you think you could be helped in a group setting, and if you are reasonably sure the topic of the course is an area where you could use some help, it might be worthwhile taking the course first before finding a therapist. The advantage here is that a course is almost always much less expensive than individual therapy. It is time-limited (often four to eight weeks) and might be all that you need to get on the right track. If no classes are offered in your area (or existing classes do not have a good reputation), if you are not sure just exactly what the problem is, if you feel that four to eight weeks of a class are unlikely to be very helpful, or if you do not want to meet in a group setting, then finding a therapist might be a better idea.

How to get the names of groups, classes and therapists

If you don't already know names of groups, classes, and therapists, you might try some of the following suggestions:

1 Ask for recommendations from your family doctor, and friends and relatives. In the United Kingdom, if you want therapy on the National Health Service, ask to be referred to a clinical psychologist.

2 Call or write to your local or national psychological association, psychiatric association, or association of social workers.

3 A university psychology department, or the psychiatric department of your area hospital, may be useful sources of the names of therapists specialising in social skills training. Write to the Head of Department and ask also for the addresses of groups and classes set up to enhance social skills. In the United Kingdom, you can contact your local Health Council, which will give you up-to-date information on all health services available in your area.

Group leaders, instructors and therapists

Selecting a good group, class, or therapist can be time-consuming and difficult. In general, the more information you have, the better able you will be to make a decision. You have the right to obtain a great deal of information about any potential group leader, instructor, or therapist. This information may be obtained from the referral person, over the phone with the individual, or at your first meeting. Although you may not feel that all this information is relevant, you will need a substantial amount of it in order to evaluate whether a particular leader, instructor, or therapist would be good for you.

Find out what qualifications a person has, and whether they are relevant to the services being offered. How much experience has that person had, and where was he or she trained? Is he or she licensed or sponsored by a reputable organization? Responsible professionals do not mind being asked about their qualifications and will freely give you any professional information you need.

Since most growth groups and classes require payment before the first meeting, the question of cost is answered before you make a commitment. Therapy, however, is generally paid for after one or more sessions. You should ask the therapist about fees before the first session, as most therapists charge for the initial visit even if you decide not to go again.

Your first meeting should always be evaluative. It does not commit you to continue with the group, class or therapist. This is your opportunity to find out whether the group or the therapist is likely to be helpful. In a group or class you may simply want to sit in and listen to what goes on, without participating. With a therapist, you should discuss the values underlying the counselling given and the goals which are particularly important to you. If the group's or therapist's views are very different from yours, find another group, class or therapist. This first meeting is when you decide whether you will feel comfortable and confident receiving help from a particular person and in a particular environment.

Questions to ask after deciding

As noted, it is important to feel that your goals and the goals of your helper match, and that you are confident that your goals are within reach. Once begun, it is important to continue to observe and question the change process. The most important question here is: Am I changing in the direction in which I want to change? If, after a reasonable length of time, you do not feel you are improving or if you are dissatisfied with your experience, there are a number of things you can do.

1 Talk with your leader, instructor, therapist. It is not uncommon for people to feel angry or frustrated at times about the helping process. If you do, you should ventilate your feelings. A good helper will be open to hearing and discussing them.

2 Get a second opinion. If you feel that the issues and problems you have raised with your group leader or instructor are not being resolved, discuss the problem with other members of the class or group. Perhaps they are having the same difficulty and together you can improve the situation. Often, the perspective of other members can be useful in

147

changing your own point of view; suddenly your problems may seem less important. If you are in therapy, you can consult another professional. Usually, the therapist you are seeing can suggest someone. If he or she objects to your consulting someone else, change to another therapist who will not object.

3 Consider dropping the group or class or changing therapists. Many people feel guilty about this. Some therapists and group leaders quite explicitly encourage this guilt, implying that there is something wrong with your wanting to stop or change. This is simply not true. If you are reasonably certain that you are not getting what you want from a group or a therapist, and if the situation seems unlikely to improve, seek help elsewhere. Good group leaders, instructors and therapists are well aware that they may not be appropriate for everyone who comes to them.

References

Introduction

Phillips, E. L., *The Social Skills Basis of Psychopathology*, New York: Grune & Stratton, 1978.

Chapter 1

Linehan, M. M., Goldfried, M. R. and Goldfried, A. P., Assertion therapy: skill training or cognitive restructuring? *Behavior Therapy*, 1979, *10*, 372–388.

Lippitt. R., Polansky, N., Redl, F. and Rosen, S. The dynamics of power. In: Cartwright, D. and Zander, A., *Group Dynamics: Research and Theory*. New York: Harper and Row, 1968.

Michener, H. A. and Suchner, R., The tactical use of social power. In: J. Tedeschi (ed.), *The Social Influence Process*. Chicago: Aldine, 1972.

Chapter 2

Bandura, A. and Walters, R. H., *Social Learning and Personality*. New York: Holt Rinehart & Winston, 1963.

Blanchard, E. B. and Epstein, L. H., *A Biofeedback Primer*. Reading, MA: Addison-Wesley, 1978.

Jones, E. E. and Nisbett, R. E., The actor and observer: divergent perceptions of the causes of behaviour. In: E. E. Jones *et al.* (eds), *Attribution: Perceiving the Causes of Behavior*. Morristown, NJ: General Learning Press, 1972.

Neisser, U., *Cognition and reality: Principles and Implications of Cognitive Psychology*. San Francisco: Freeman, 1976.

Schwartz, G. E. and Shapiro, D., Biofeedback and essential hypertension: current findings and theoretical concerns. In: Birk (ed.), *Biofeedback: Behavioral Medicine*. New York: Grune & Stratton, 1973.

Skinner, B. F., *The Technology of Teaching*. New York: Appleton-Century-Crofts, 1968.

Thorndike, E. L., Animal intelligence. *Psychological Review Monograph Supplement*, 1898, *8*.

Chapter 3

Adams, G. R. and Huston, T. L., Social perception of middle-aged persons varying in physical attractiveness. *Developmental Psychology*, 1975, *11*, 650–658.

Beck, A., *Cognitive Therapy of Depression*. Wiley, 1979.

Bull, R. and Stevens, J., The relationship between ratings of persons' facial appearance and ratings of their conversation. *Language and Speech*, 1981, *24*, 285–291.

Bull, R. and Stevens, J., The effects of facial disfiguration on helping behaviour. *Italian Journal of Psychology*, 1981, *8*, 25–33.

Cavior, N. and Dorecki, P. R., Physical attractiveness and popularity among fifth-grade boys. Paper presented at the S.W. Psychological Association, Austin, Texas, 1969.

Combs, M. L. and Slaby, D. A., Social skills training with children. In: Kasdin, A. E. and Lahey, B. B., *Advances in Clinical Child Psychology*, Vol. I. Plenum Press, 1977.

Dion, K., Berscheid, E. and Walster, E., What is beautiful is good. *Journal of Personality and Social Psychology*, 1972, *24*, 207–213.

Ellis, A., *Reason and Emotion in Psychotherapy*. New York: Stuart, 1962.

Feldman-Summers, S. and Kiesler, S., Those who are number two try harder: the effect of sex on attributions of causality. *Journal of Personality and Social Psychology*, 1974, *30*

Glasgow, R. and Arkowitz, H., The behavioural assessment of male and female social competence in dyadic heterosexual interactions. *Behavior Therapy*, 1975, *8*, 488–498.

Goldman, W. and Lewis, P., Beautiful is good: evidence the physically unattractive are more socially skilful. *Journal of Experimental Social Psychology*, 1977, *13*, 125–130.

Lewinshon, P., Mischel, W., Chaplin, W. and Barton, R., Social competence and depression: the role of illusory self-perceptions. *Journal of Abnormal Psychology*, 1980, *89*, 203–212.

Chapter 4

Argyle, M., *Social Interaction*. Methuen, 1969.
Lewinshon, P., *et al.*, *Control Your Depression*. San Francisco: Spectrum, 1978.
Orvis, B. R., *et al.*, Attributional conflict in young couples. In: Harvey, J. H., Ickes, W. and Kidd, R. F. (eds.), *New Directions in Attribution Research*, Vol. 1. Hillsdale, NJ: Laurence Earlbaum Assoc., 1975.
Rehm, L., *Behavior Therapy for Depression: Present Status and Future Direction*. Academic Press, 1981.
Spivak, G., Platt, J. J. and Shure, D. B., *The Problem-solving Approach to Adjustment*. San Francisco: Jossey-Bass, 1976.

Chapter 5

Al Issa, I., *The Psychopathology of Women*. Prentice Hall, 1980.
Bellack, A. S., *et al.*, Role-play tests for the assessment of social skills: are they valid? *Behavior Therapy*, 1978, *9*, 448–461.
Caplan, P. J., Beyond the box score: a boundary condition for sex differences in aggression and achievement striving. In: Maher, B. (ed.), *Advances in Experimental Personality Research*, Vol. 9. Academic Press, 1979.
Jacobson, N. S. and Mangolin, G., *Marital Therapy: Strategies Based on Social Learning and Behavior Exchange Principles*. New York: Brunner Mazel, 1979.
Linehan, M. M., Brown, S. H., Nielsen, S. L., Olny, K. and McFall, R. M., The effectiveness of three styles of assertion. Paper presented at Association for the Advancement of Behavior Therapy meeting, New York, 1980.
Smith, M. J., *'When I Say No I Feel Guilty'*. Bantam Books, 1975.

Stuart, R. B., *Helping Couples Change: A Social Learning Approach to Marital Therapy.* New York: Guildford Press, 1980.

Chapter 6

Byrne, D., *The Attraction Paradigm.* Academic Press, 1971.

Cattell, R. B. and Nesselrode, J. R., Likeness and completeness theories examined by sixteen personality factor measures on stably and unstably married couples. *Journal of Personality and Social Psychology*, 1967, 7, 351–361.

Festinger, L. Schachter, S. and Back, K., *Social Pressures in Informal Groups: a Study of a Housing Community.* New York: Harper and Row, 1950.

Jones, E. E. and Wortman, C., *Ingratiation: an Attributional Approach.* Morristown, NJ: General Learning Press, 1973.

Kelly, J. A., *et al.*, Improving heterosocial conversation skills of male psychiatric patients through a small group training procedure. *Behavior Therapy*, 1980, 11, 179–188.

Krietman, N., *et al.*, Neurosis and marital interaction in manifest psychological interaction. *British Journal of Psychiatry*, 1971, 119, 243–252.

Kupke, T. E., *et al.*, Selection of heterosocial skills criterion-related validity. *Behavior Therapy*, 1979, 10, 327–335.

Minkin, L., *et al.*, The social validation and training of conversation skills. *Journal of Applied Behavioral Analysis*, 1976, 9, 127–139.

Stuckert, R. P., Role perception and marital satisfaction: a configural approach. *Marriage and Family Living*, 1963, 25, 415–419.

Chapter 7

Bandura, A. Self-efficacy: toward a unifying theory of behavioral change. *Advances in Behavior Research and Therapy*, 1978, 1, 139–161.

Bem, D. Self-perception theory. In: Berkowitz, L. (ed.), *Advances in Experimental Social Psychology*, Vol. 6. New York: Academic Press, 1972.

Berscheid, E. and Walster, E. H., *Interpersonal Attraction*. Reading, MA: Addison-Wesley, 1978.

Bower, S. A. and Bower, G. H., *Asserting Yourself*. Reading, MA: Addison-Wesley, 1976.

Brink, J. H., Effect of interpersonal communication on attraction. *Journal of Personality and Social Psychology*, 1977, *35*, 783–790.

Chervie, G. J., *et al.*, *Self-disclosure*. San Francisco: Jossey-Bass, 1979.

Festinger, L., *A Theory of Cognitive Dissonance*. Stanford, Calif.: Stanford University Press, 1957.

Gergen, K. J., *The Concept of Self*. New York: Holt, Rinehart and Winston, 1971.

Novak, D. W. and Lerner, M. J., Rejection as a function of perceived similarity. *Journal of Personality and Social Psychology*, *9*, 147–152.

Percell, L. P., Berwick, P. T. and Beigel, A. The effects of assertive training on self-concept and anxiety. *Archives of General Psychiatry*, 1974, 502–504.

Styker, S., Role-taking accuracy and adjustment. *Sociometry*, 1957, *20*, 286–296.

Videbeck, R. Self-conception and the reaction of others. *Sociometry*, 1960, *23*, 351–362.

Chapter 8

Asch, S., Studies of independence and conformity: a minority of one against a unanimous majority. *Psychology Monographs*, 1956, *79*, No. 9.

Bales, R. F. and Slater, P., Role differentiation in small decision-making groups. In: Parsons, T. and Bales, R. F. (eds), *Family, Socialization and Interaction Processes*. Glencoe Ill: Free Press, 1955.

Festinger, L., Pepitone, A. and Newcomb, T., Some consequences of de-individuation in a group. *Journal of Abnormal and Social Psychology*, 1952, *47*, 382–389.

Fiedler, F. E., *Leadership.* New York: General Learning Press, 1971.

Gintner, G. and Linskold, S., Rate of participation and expertise as factor influencing leader choice. *Journal of Personality and Social Psychology*, 1975, *32*, 1085–1089.

Schachter, S., Deviation, rejection and communication. *Journal of Abnormal and Social Psychology*, 1951, *46*, 190–207.

Sorrentino, R. M. and Boutillier, R. G., The effect of quantity and quality of verbal interaction on ratings of leadership ability. *Journal of Experimental Social Psychology*, 1975, *11*, 403–411.

Zimbardo, P., The psychological power and pathology of imprisonment. Statement prepared for US House of Representatives Committee on the Judiciary (Subcommittee No. 3, Robert Kastimeyer, Chairman, hearings on prison reform). Unpublished paper, Stanford University, 1971.

Chapter 9

Exline, R. V., Explorations in the process of person perception: visual interaction in relation to competition, sex and the need for affiliation. *Journal of Personality*, 1963, *31*, 1–20.

Fischer, J. D., *et al.*, *Hands Touching*, 1976, *39*, 416–421.

Hall, E. T., *The Hidden Dimension: Man's Use of Space in Public and Private.* New York: Bodley Head, 1969.

Jourard, S., An exploratory study of body accessibility. *British Journal of Social and Clinical Psychology*, 1966, *5*, 221–231.

Kagan, J. and Lewis, M., Studies of attention in the human infant. *Menill-Palmer Quarterly*, 1965, *2*, 95–122.

Linehan, M. M. and Egan, K. J., Assertion training for women. In: Bellack, A. S. and Hersen M. (eds), *Research and Practice of Social Skills Training.* New York: Plenum, 1979.

Morris, D., *Manwatching.* London: Cape, 1977.

Nicosia, G. J. and Aiello, R. J., Effects of body contact

on reactions to crowding. Paper read at meeting of American Psychological Association, Washington DC, 1976.

Chapter 10

Bandura, A., Self-efficacy: towards a unifying theory of behaviour change. *Psychological Review*, 1977, *84*, 191–215.

Bower, S. A. and Bower, G. H., *Asserting Yourself*. Reading, MA: Addison-Wesley, 1976.

Index

M

N

O

P

R